GAIL JONES

Gail Jones teaches cinema, literary and cultural studies at the University of Western Australia. She is also the author of two books of short stories: *The House of Breathing* (1992) and *Fetish Lives* (1997), and four novels: *Black Mirror* (2002), *Sixty Lights* (2004), *Dreams of Speaking* (2006) and *Sorry* (2007). Her work is widely translated and the recipient of several literary awards.

For my mother

AUSTRALIAN SCREEN CLASSICS

the piano
GAIL JONES

CURRENCY PRESS,
SYDNEY

AUSTRALIAN FILM COMMISSION
NATIONAL FILM & SOUND ARCHIVE

First published by Currency Press Pty Ltd and the Australian Film Commission in 2007.

Currency Press Pty Ltd
PO Box 2287, Strawberry Hills
NSW 2012 Australia
enquiries@currency.com.au
www.currency.com.au

National Film and Sound Archive
A division of the Australian Film Commission
GPO Box 2002, Canberra
ACT 2601 Australia
www.nfsa.afc.gov.au

Copyright © Gail Jones, 2007

Copying for Educational Purposes: The Australian *Copyright Act* 1968 allows a maximum of one chapter or 10% of this book, whichever is the greater, to be copied by any educational institution for its educational purposes provided that the educational institution (or the body that administers it) has given a remuneration notice to Copyright Agency Limited (CAL) under the Act. For details of the CAL licence for educational institutions, please contact CAL: 19/157 Liverpool Street, Sydney NSW 2000; tel: (02) 9394 7600; fax: (02) 9394 7601; email: info@copyright.com.au

Copying for Other Purposes: Except as permitted under the Act, for example a fair dealing for the purposes of study, research, criticism or review, no part of this book may be reproduced, stored in a retrieval system, or transmitted in any form or by any means without prior written permission. All inquiries should be made to the publisher at the above address.

In accordance with the requirement of the Australian Media and Entertainment Arts Alliance, Currency Press has made every effort to identify, and gain permission of, the artists who appear in the photographs which illustrate this book.

Every effort has been made to trace and acknowledge copyright. However, should any infringement have occurred, the publishers tend their apologies and invite copyright holders to contact them.

Australian Screen Classics series: ISSN 1447-557X

National Library of Australia—Cataloguing-in-Publication Data:

Jones, Gail, 1955- .
    The piano.
    Bibliography.
    ISBN 9780868197999.
    1. Piano (Motion picture). 2. Campion, Jane. I. Title.
    791.4372

Cover design by Kate Florance, Currency Press

Front cover shows Holly Hunter as Ada and Anna Paquin as Flora.

Typeset by Currency Press in Iowan Old Style roman 9.5 pt.

Printed by Ligare Pty Ltd, Riverwood, NSW

All photographs within the text are from *The Piano* © JAN CHAPMAN Productions – CIBY 2000 / 1992.

AUSTRALIAN SCREEN CLASSICS

JANE MILLS
Series Editor

Our national cinema plays a vital role in our cultural heritage and in showing us at least something of what it is to be Australian. But the picture can get blurred by unruly forces such as competing artistic aims, inconstant personal tastes, political vagaries, constantly changing priorities in screen education and training, and technological innovations and market forces.

When these forces remain unconnected, the result can be an artistically impoverished cinema and audiences who are disinclined to seek out and derive pleasure from a diverse range of films, including Australian ones.

This series is a part of screen culture which is the glue needed to stick these forces together. It's the plankton in the moving image food chain that feeds the imagination of our filmmakers and their audiences. It's what makes sense of the opinions, memories, responses, knowledge and exchange of ideas about film.

Above all, screen culture is informed by a *love* of cinema. And it has to be carefully nurtured if we are to understand and appreciate the aesthetic, moral, intellectual and sentient value of our national cinema.

Australian Screen Classics will match some of our best-loved films with some of our most distinguished writers and thinkers, drawn from the worlds of culture, criticism and politics. All we ask of our writers is that they feel passionate about the films they choose. Through these thoughtful, elegantly-written books, we hope that screen culture will work its sticky magic and introduce more audiences to Australian cinema.

Jane Mills is a Senior Research Associate at the Australian Film, Television & Radio School, a member of the Board of Directors of Cinewest, and is the recipient of a scholarship at the Centre for Cultural Research, University of Western Australia. She is currently writing a book about the relationship between global and local cinemas.

CONTENTS

Australian Screen Classics	v
Acknowledgments	viii
1. The Sea, The Sea	1
2. Too Strangely Near: the Romantic Plot	6
3. Beginnings: Touchy-feely	13
4. The Colonial Economy	20
5. Hush-hush-hush: Silence, Words, Music	34
6. Erotics, Feeling and the Masculine	43
7. The Mutilation	54
8. The Uncanny Child	61
9. The Three Endings	66
Notes	73
Bibliography	79
Filmography	83
Credits	84

ACKNOWLEDGMENTS

The author wishes to thank the Series Editor, Jane Mills, for her intelligent, sophisticated and clever attention to this text and for sharing generously her cinephilic pleasure from which such labour derives. I also wish to thank the students at the University of Western Australia with whom, over several years, I have discussed *The Piano*; their insights and provocations form part of my reading of this film. I am also grateful the artists and academics at Camargo Foundation, Cassis, who patiently watched a screening with me, and to Lauren, Michelle and Kyra for their enthusiastic engagement at a final viewing. Special thanks to Claire Grady and Kate Florance of Currency Press for their enormous patience, professionalism and intellectual support.

The Series Editor would like to thank the Australian Film, Television & Radio School, especially the unfailingly supportive librarians, and everyone at the Dr What video store of Bondi Junction.

# 1

THE SEA, THE SEA

Jane Campion once spoke of a movie, *Ebb*, which she considered, but never made:

> It was an imaginary story about a country where one day the sea leaves, never returns, and the way in which the people have to find a spiritual solution to this problem. The natural world had become artificial and unpredictable and the film spoke about faith and doubt. The inhabitants of this country had developed a certain form of spirituality, hearing voices, having visions.[1]

There is something strangely compelling in this mini-narrative, and in oblique ways it speaks of the concerns of *The Piano*. A movie premised, hypothetically at least, on loss and redemption, on a spiritual struggle to deal with the bewildering subtraction of something that had seemed otherwise essential, *The Piano*, also, attempts to 'solve' certain conditions of absence and estrangement, the world made unfamiliar, the challenge of recovery, of forms of damage that can only be negotiated by visions. Curiously, too, *The Piano* works with a sensibility of *immersion*, as if in a dialectical gesture willing the *flow* that *Ebb* hypothetically cancelled. According to cinematographer, Stuart Dryburgh,

> Part of the director's brief was that we would echo the film's element of underwater in the bush. 'Bottom of the fish tank' was the description we used for ourselves to define what we were looking for. So we played it murky green-blue.[2]

What symbolic sea-space is this? Why the wish for a fish-tank filter of murky aquamarine? And what directorial command, therefore, to obliterate visually, if only in certain scenes or as a suggestive and subliminal trace, the necessary division of earth and ocean? The nineteenth-century critic John Ruskin once famously described the sea as 'an irreconcilable mixture of fury and formalism', expressing exasperation at its representational challenge. What is worth exploring, I think, are the ways in which *The Piano* is hinged on just this kind of contradiction: an aesthetic of both containment and excess, the rhythmical unrolling of images, recurring with wave-like regularity, but also their overlapping, an interior turbulence, a sense of spill into dimensions of sublimity and vastness. Every movie, of course, is a *motion* picture, a system of fluctuation and 'continuous mobility'.[3] What is interesting here is the wave-motion of certain movies, the forms in which they rehearse the making and unmaking within the frame, their spatial and temporal logic, their manufacture of cinematic coherence, their roiling to the shore of a more-or-less specific conclusion.[4]

Revising *Ebb*, the *look* of *The Piano* is thus often submarine: there is a watery quality to many of the shots, and New Zealand, the principal setting, is remade as a perilous and drenching heterotopia, a place not for touristic or colonial satisfactions of the picturesque, but somewhere other-worldly, deep, bluish, strange, somewhere, indeed, that might ultimately suck one under, or dissolve the self into place in disturbing ways.[5] Described by one writer as 'a muddy, glutinous (and) fluid landscape', it might also therefore be read as *feminised*.[6] The sea is recurrently evoked, prayed to in a Maori ritual, photographed as bands of light and dark, or thundering dramatically at the limits of the visible world.

Add to this Michael Nyman's famously hypnotic score, which swells and rises, ebbs and flows, saturates the crucial scenes in an irresistible tonal wash. The soundtrack, that is to say, is also fluid; its motifs recur in a kind of compulsive repetition, based in part on the composer's knowledge of the forms of baroque rounds and canons. The music crests and falls and superimposes; it moves with broad tidal sweep, just as waves do. The climax of the narrative, such as it is, is the heroine's near-drowning. She descends to expressionist film-making, lapis light and a lush enveloping score, seeming to go down and down, way into shadowy depths, so that her ascent and recovery seem almost a continuity mistake. (More of that later.) And the movie ends, as viewers may puzzle-headedly recall, with an image of the heroine, Ada, suspended beneath the ocean, swaying, darkly obscure, within light-shot currents. Her dress oddly resembles a domed sea creature, ballooning around her. She is filmed from below, as if the camera has finally sunk to the ocean floor, as if that is where the directorial and cinematic consciousness of *The Piano* finally comes to rest. It is *drowned, but seeing*. There is then a cut-to-black, and a quote from *Silence*, a poem by the English poet Thomas Hood (1799–1845), one which initially was to have been used in *Ebb*.[7]

> There is a silence where hath been no sound,
> There is a silence where no sound may be,
> In the cold grave—under the deep, deep sea.

In one of the boldest conceptual moves in *The Piano*, the deep, deep sea that is the destination of this movie is paradoxically both the emblem of the persistence of desire (life) and the loss of desire (death). The voice-over speaks both alive and *posthumously*, claiming the territory Roland Barthes once identified as the impossible space of pure fiction, the 'scandal' of enunciation where none should truly exist.[8] The sense of oceanic conclusion, of altered perception, of the beautiful and terrifying reversibility of things, are all contained in the last image and the ripple-lines of quotation that follow it.

So how do we arrive at such a moment of spooky audacity? At such a haunting, deliquescent, point of view? How has this second *Ebb*, or this putative *Flow*, returned the ocean in a post-colonial narrative? And what does it mean to align passion with natural forces, to situate subjects in the drag and undertow of altered states and rhythms? In this essay I wish to address the physical quirkiness of *The Piano* (its representations of the body and sense experience), and to investigate its peculiar, and peculiarly insistent, metaphysics. This is a movie much written about—sometimes in depressingly reductive and schematic ways—yet it carries an

The stranded piano.

aesthetically distinctive poetics, even as it rehearses familiar genres with mostly familiar movie stars. Famously, too, *The Piano* inspires adoration, sometimes to the point of gushy devotion, so I wish also to examine its remarkable emotional appeal. Its popular success—as the winner of three Academy Awards in 1994 and the prestigious *Palme d'Or* at Cannes in 1993 (shared with Chen Kaige's *Farewell My Concubine*)—has in many ways occluded the formal qualities of the movie, and presented it, predictably, in more market-driven terms: the virtuosity of the stars, the sexual plot, the dank exoticism of darkest New Zealand. Early reviewers sometimes offered appalled condemnation: Stanley Kauffmann calls it 'an over-wrought, hollowly symbolic glob of glutinous nonsense' and says:

> '[I] haven't seen a sillier film about a woman and her piano since John Huston's *The Unforgiven* (1960) in which Lillian Gish had her piano carried out into the front yard so she could play Mozart to pacify attacking Indians.'[9]

More often, however, the reception was one of extraordinary praise, often couched in highly emotive terms: 'For a while I could not think, let alone write about *The Piano* without shaking. Precipitating a flood of feelings, *The Piano* demands as much a physical and emotional response as an intellectual one ... I wanted to rush at the screen and shout and scream.'[10] Such strong identifications and fervent responses have formed the basis of both feminist and anti-feminist criticism and been the reason for the film's acceptance or rejection. Acknowledging its emotional appeal, another critic writes: 'The film gives *reason* nothing to do.'[11] So in this essay I shall impersonate the visitor from the land of *Ebb*, who sees the movie for the very first time. I shall assess its unearthly and controversial visions, its attractive powers, and its capacity to alienate and to entrance.

2
TOO STRANGELY NEAR: THE ROMANTIC PLOT

The story is well known. Our heroine, Ada McGrath (Holly Hunter), a mute Scottish woman, is sent by her father to marry a man, Alisdair Stewart (Sam Neill), in colonial New Zealand. It is perhaps 1860, judging by the costumes. She has a young daughter, Flora (Anna Paquin), and there is some unexplained, possible shameful, history she carries. Certainly it seems likely that Flora is 'illegitimate', so that the marriage is marked at the outset as opportunistic, as one of 'convenience'. Apart from her silent condition, Ada is unusual in that she exhibits a fierce ardour for, and even identification with, her Broadwood piano, the prosthetic object, as it were, for her missing voice.[12] Mother, daughter and piano are all shipped to the colony to be collected by Stewart, and inserted into the second neat triangle of a ready-made family. Instead, however, the domestic plot is overturned when Stewart trades his new wife's piano to George Baines (Harvey Keitel), a colonist with Maori sympathies. Ada is seduced (or perhaps self-traded) into a relationship with Baines, a curiously passive, quiet and indecisive figure, in order to recover possession of the piano. The interior action takes place between Stewart's house, Baines's

THE PIANO

house, and 'the mission house', a place where the Reverend (Ian Mune), Aunt Morag (Kerry Walker) and Nessie (Genevieve Lemon)—all of whom bear an unclear relation to Stewart—uphold standards of strict Scottish rectitude by which the illicit lovers will be judged. A further triangle develops, the third term of which once again is Flora. Her presence is perhaps the most volatile in the movie: she has voice, energy and wilfully mischievous agency. She shouts, runs, performs, betrays and displays a ventriloquising relationship with her mother that curiously joins and 'weds' them. In the collision of passions that follows, Stewart attacks Ada, severing one of her fingers with an axe, and then confronts Baines, threatening but releasing him. The resolution is fractured and complicated—of which more later—but Baines, Ada and Flora create an entirely new family, settled together in the South Island township of Nelson. It is a story resolved romantically, but also with a certain complicating and confusing mysticism.

Initially called 'The Piano Lesson', then 'The Sleep of Reason', earlier versions of the script were more violent and tempestuous. There were more fingers hacked off, and Baines kills Stewart. The script, that is to say, moved away from exaggerated and dramatic violence, towards threat, to interiority and psychological drama, and to all that resides in the allusion to Goya's famous etching, *The Sleep of Reason Produces Monsters*: irrational release, the night-time other-side of dream, sexual excess and unhinging madness. (Goya's etching is presumed to be a self-portrait. It depicts a man collapsed asleep at his writing desk—not in bed—with ominous big-eyed, owl-like creatures winging around him. This image invokes the interpenetration of dreaming and writing and the cruel capacity of visions to torment and to arrive unbidden.)

In interviews, Campion has frequently been asked about the sources and inspiration for *The Piano*, and her responses are remarkably uniform. Significantly, she cites not cinematic precedents, but nineteenth-century literary romance melodramas. *Wuthering Heights* appears to be an especial favourite, along with novels by Henry James and George Eliot, texts like Kate Chopin's *The Awakening* and the poetry of Emily Dickinson. The novel version of *The Piano* (co-written by Jane Campion and Kate Pullinger in 1994) is prefaced with the following quote:

> Today I will seek not the shadowy region;
> Its unsustaining vastness waxes drear;
> And visions rising, legion after legion,
> Bring the unreal world too strangely near.

Taken from Emily Bronte's *Stanza* (1846), this may be read as the director's own literary-critical gloss on her work: it expresses both an attraction to the visionary and a reluctance wholly to entertain it; the shadowy region hovers as a possibly pathological enticement to Victorian women bent on artistic or emotional escapism. The mode of Gothicism may be implicitly cinematic: with its imagistic repertoire of wild spaces, supernatural occurrences, extravagant announcements and scenes of out-of-control passion on dark-and-stormy nights. The high romanticism of the Gothic, too, often construed in sexualised encounters, fits well with the emotional and fantasy regimes of cinema. In an interesting argument, the film critic Dana Polan calls *The Piano* 'reverse Gothic'.[13] He refers to the scenario in which erotic fulfilment can only occur outside marriage: the 'intended' partner is revealed as inadequate, and a 'rival' contests the mainstream ideology of matrimony by offering a kind of authentification of passion. This seems to be an accurate description of both *The Piano* and *Wuthering Heights*. It is the revaluing of illicit passion, then, that is at the centre of the 'reverse Gothic', not the figure of the husband, as in earlier cinematic versions (of which Hitchcock's *Rebecca* (1941) and

THE PIANO

The Romantic Heroine: Ada.

Suspicion (1941) are exemplary). Another reading insists it is the refiguring of masculinity in *The Piano*, that is to say the eroticising of the male figure who is marginal, working class, illiterate and emotionally vulnerable, that marks the movie's distinctive take on the Gothic.[14] Stewart, whom one would expect to be sexually dominating (symbolically allied with British colonialism, patriarchy, ownership and control) is disqualified sexually and rendered pathetic and impotent. Played with self-conscious unease by Sam Neill, who is more conventionally cast in heroic or romantic leads, he is a figure of compromised value and insecure sexuality. The Gothicism, then, is in any case unorthodox. For all its tropes of jealousy, violence and moody feeling, it has at its centre an enthrallment (as one expects in the Gothic), but it is between two figures set apart by forms of silencing and linked more to the expressive body, than to any system of power.

Campion's reference to literary precedents is so repetitious as to betoken a kind of writerly ambition:

> I am attracted to Romantic literature and I wanted to contribute to the genre. I think especially of *Wuthering Heights*, and for poetry Blake, Tennyson and Byron. I went to the village where Emily Bronte was brought up. I walked on the moor and wanted to retain the atmosphere. But it was very evident I didn't want to make a transposition of *Wuthering Heights*, because I don't think the story could be told today; it's a saga that extends over two generations and moreover I'm not English. I belong to a colonial culture and I had to invent my own fiction.[15]

In public interviews—of which there are many—Campion is conspicuously more likely to mention a literary heritage than a filmic one. Cinematically, she has stated allegiance to Antonioni and Bertolucci (and European cinema in general) but asked directly about films with which she has an affinity, she alludes vaguely to David Lynch (without citing a title) and John Huston (citing only his adaptation of Flannery O'Connor's novel, *Wise Blood*). She also mentions Marguerite Duras, but it is clearly her novels, not her movies, which Campion takes as important. The feature preceding *The Piano*, a biographical tribute to the New Zealand author Janet Frame, *An Angel at my Table* (1990), and that immediately following, an adaptation of Henry James's *The Portrait of a Lady* (1996), confirm the pre-eminence of the literary imaginary in Campion's film-making. The 'novelisation' of *The Piano* is further evidence of the wish for her text to be inserted into a literary tradition. Unfortunately, the book is dull, tonally flat and without the enigma of muteness and patrimony that lends inquisitive pleasure to a viewing of the film. In the novel, Ada's muteness is banally explained (her father rebuked her for spilling sugar on the table, so she decided, in a fit of bizarrely obstinate petulance, never again to speak), as is the fatherhood of Flora (a single occasion of lovemaking with her piano teacher who bore the name of Delwar Hauser), and Stewart's history (as a failed romantic) and Baines' (as a whaler). All are 'settled', as it were, revealed and made explicable. It carries none of the charge of the filmic narrative which sensibly leaves such matters 'silent'.[16] This is not to say that the novel is 'unfaithful'; but it does draw attention, paradoxically, to the virtuosity of the film, in particular to its reliance on the rhetoric of the image, rather than explanation, and the centrality of the soundtrack in constructing an idiosyncratic emotional dimension.

The originality of the story has been publicly acclaimed—Campion won the Academy Award in 1993 for Best Original Screenplay. But it has also been fiercely contested and repudiated. In the 1920's the New Zealand novelist Jane Mander wrote a novel called *The Story of a New Zealand River*, which also dealt with a woman, her daughter and a piano arriving in nineteenth century New Zealand, and in which the woman begins an extramarital affair. Since Campion concedes she knew the text, a certain controversy attaches to the origins of the story of *The Piano*.[17] That it is a 'literary' movie, in any case, is undisputed.

3
BEGINNINGS: TOUCHY-FEELY

A glorious opening image: the world stained bloody pink, seen through an oddly luminous, and not-quite-opaque, screen of fingers. Not an object but a subject, the protagonist's point of view is at first represented, mysteriously, as vision *through* her hands. This unusual viewing position—perplexing, visually confusing, impaired by the physical barrier of the body—has been used by the film theorist Vivian Sobchack to argue that the movie sets up a 'carnal modality'.[18] It is a movie, she argues, less about vision than touch; it references reading-through-the-body, what Laura Marks calls 'haptic visuality'.[19] Sobchack describes her first encounter with this scene:

> As I watched *The Piano*'s opening moments—in that first shot, before I even knew there was an Ada and before I saw her from my side of her vision (that is, before I watched her rather than her vision)—something seemingly extraordinary happened. Despite my 'almost blindness', the 'unrecognisable blur', and resistance of the image to my eyes, my fingers knew what I was looking at—and this before the objective reverse shot that followed to put those fingers in their proper place (that is, to put them where they could be seen objectively rather than subjectively 'looked through'.[20]

This is not just a claim for the sensuous power of the movie, but for its capacity to implicate the viewer's body. Sobchack's rhapsodic account of the opening is elaborated into an entire ontology; cinema can create, she argues, a *cinesthetic* subject, one which, experiencing *synesthesia* (the mutual pun is important), confounds sense perception and makes us feel by seeing. This is a very large claim for the opening scene, but also a fascinating one for understanding the adoration (possibly gendered) that attaches to this movie. The viewer here is granted not only vision but an entire 'sensorium', just as, it may be perversely argued, we might find ourselves sexually stimulated watching pornography (a somewhat less lyrical link Sobchack does not go on to make). In any case, the fleeting sensation of embodiment, so early established, remains like a memory of integrity within the film: only gradually do we learn that this film is indeed about touch, about what fingers can do, what sounds they can make, what intimacies and violence they might know of and suffer.

The term for this model of cinema viewing is phenomenology: it directs us to consider relations of inner (consciousness) and outer (embodiment); it emphasises sense experience (seeing, hearing and so on) and how we deal with the manifold 'phenomena' of the world. Including both the viewer and the characters on the screen, it also addresses ideas of perception and attention and tries to account for the role of imagination, desire and will in founding our personal sense of self. Since Campion's films so frequently link inner and outer in this way, her work has attracted this kind of analysis. Questions are raised about whether she presents a particular view of the body and whether there is something distinctively female in her filmmaking.

THE PIANO

Sound-tracking the veiny red pillars of fingers, there is gently swelling music, a kind of inchoate overture, then a voice-over spoken in a mild Scottish accent and sounding rather childish:

> The voice you hear is not my speaking voice, but my mind's voice.
>
> I have not spoken since I was six years old. No one knows why, not even me. My father says it is a dark talent and the day I take it into my head to stop breathing will be my last.
>
> Today he married me to a man I've not yet met. Soon my daughter and I will join him in his own country. My husband says my muteness does not bother him. He writes and hark this: God loves dumb creatures, so why not he!
>
> Were good he had God's patience for silence affects everyone in the end. The strange thing is that I don't think myself silent, that is, because of my piano. I shall miss it on the journey.

The camera swings upwards, looking down upon Ada rising from beneath a tree on a comfortable estate, and this too initiates symbolically one of the crucial devices of the movie—to relativise seeing, to make perspective unstable between inner and outer lives, to look upon the silent woman, self-enclosed, self-possessed, who has decided from that moment to retreat from all telling.

But what of the prefatory 'speech'? This is one of the most intriguing openings to a movie I know of, not only because it begins with a subjective shot and partial and screened seeing but because of the density of enigmatic information we are given to begin with. The distinction between the 'speaking voice' and the 'mind's voice' would seem to be the standard ruse of the voice-over, however Campion does not make use of this essentially explanatory device. Another filmmaker, less subtle, might have used it throughout the movie to tell the audience more securely what Ada is thinking, but after the opening the voice retreats and she is given back the privacy that confirms her mystery.

'Voice' is problematic because Ada is an elective mute (*I have not spoken since I was six years old. No one knows why, not even me*). and this too is re-valued. Mutism here is not a deficiency but an act of exemplary will, not an index of trauma, apparently, but of forthright decisiveness. It is a *talent*—the word recalling the parable of the talents in the Bible, referring to the obligation to use, not bury, whatever might be given to one as value. Against this private economy, linked explicitly to childhood, is the Victorian marriage and the power of the father (*he married me to a man*) and this essential contest—between inner worth and patriarchal economy, between child-knowing and adult-knowing—governs the movie. Ada is wry (*hark this*); she knows her distant husband has already decided the value of 'dumb', but is also aware that silence is an incalculable and weird force: *silence affects everyone in the end*. So we have, in a few words, the disavowal of speech, its replacement by the piano, and the vague contiguity of child and bride. The images that follow—the brief Scottish episodes of the movie—show Flora sitting on a pony, then flying up a gloomy corridor on roller skates, the cutting away of the skates by her mother (the first of many blades and cuttings in a movie which consolidates its imagery), and Ada playing a farewell on her voice-substitute piano, only to be interrupted by an elderly maid who drags her hand along a pearly glass screen to produce a kind of imagistic 'halt' sign.

What follows is a wave-shift in terms of the movie's aesthetics. The hand on the domestic-interior screen and the look of rebuke from the maid cuts to Ada's reaction and then, with a

THE PIANO

Ada and Flora arrive in New Zealand.

frisson of disorientation, to an amplified and abstracted underwater shot. Again, an impossible—or perhaps inhuman—point of view is evoked. We are looking up at the bottom of a boat slicing the ocean into elongated, shiny skeins. The next shot is of dark hands reaching upwards for Ada and Flora as they are physically conveyed to the beach in New Zealand. Ada is shown balanced precariously at the start of her new life, her black ribbons are tossing, she looks afraid, apprehensive, as hands reach up to support her in a fan of willing fingers. After this comes one of the most beautiful images in *The Piano*: filmed in long-shot, Flora and Ada are carried on the shoulders of the sailors, held aloft above the crashing waves. They are transformed by collective labour into composite creatures and pass like multi-limbed

AUSTRALIAN SCREEN CLASSICS

Transforming symbols: shadow play and the hooped skirt.

THE PIANO

mythical figures above the churning foam and silver stripes of a rowdy ocean. Lasting only a few seconds, it is a radical vision of arrival, and of being held against the forces of engulfment. (In the screenplay there is this odd note: 'We should be forgiven if this woman seems a sacrificial offering as the bay they carry her to is completely uninhabited.')[21] There are shots of the beach, sailors talking and pissing, Flora keeled over and doubled up, vomiting on the sand. Ada watches the overflowing ocean stream between her feet. Then we see the deposition of the piano on a shimmery tidal sheet. It too has arrived, visually indelible as the shape by which the movie summarises its nature/culture conundrums. Also worthy of note is the attention to what is called the abject body, the body in its disorder (vomiting, pissing, being invaded by water) that contributes to the sense overall that this movie is focussed on embodiment and its uncomfortable contradictions.

The credits end here, with an object already made symbolic. And in a movie composed so carefully of competing discursive systems, it is the location of the piano, and who is touching it, that will hereafter enable us to track the shifting systems of desire within the plot. For now, Ada and Flora are abandoned by the sailors to the elements. Darkness falls and the two shelter inside one of Ada's whalebone petticoats. Frailly contained, poetically isolated, they make a little community of two in their protective space. Interestingly, too, the petticoat produces a kind of screen or theatre. Flora creates hand-shadows on its concave sides, setting up a motif that will gather force as the movie develops.

4
THE COLONIAL ECONOMY

What of the 'background' to this movie? Imprecise in its historical moment, *The Piano* is nevertheless clearly situated in the colonial period of New Zealand and the markers of colonialist and intercultural experience necessarily pre-empt and predispose the sexual plot. New Zealand (Aotearoa) is a contested site, the history of which confirms indigenous Maori as by no means passively acquiescent to colonial rule but shrewdly adaptive, selectively appropriative and heroically self-fashioning.[22] Depopulated and ravaged by European diseases to which they had little immunity, subjected to Christian missionaries from as early as 1814, internally damaged by the musket trade which disastrously altered their forms of traditional warfare, Maori were in fact remarkably resilient in the face of an inordinate invasion. The total number of Pakeha (European white) settlers in 1840 was a little over 2,000.[23] But as historian Michael King points out, the growth of the colonising community was unusually swift: 'By 1858 they would outnumber Maori by approximately 3,000, 59,000 to 56,000. And by 1881 there would be around 500,000 of them'.[24] In forty years, therefore, the population shifted: Maori lands were expropriated, alienated or traded, the ecology of the islands was drastically changed, and the cultural landscape was irrevocably reconstructed.

For all the debates around bodies, subjectivities and erotics that *The Piano* entails, one must pause and ask: what of the Maori bodies? Are relations between Maori and Pakeha justly represented? And what effect does the colonial economy of value—that of profit, trade and domination—have in establishing the primary sexual relationship of the movie?

Consider this establishing scene, just a few minutes into the movie. Maori are moving slowly through the blue-filtered submarine forest, merging with it, fading, appearing indistinct. The colonist in their company, Stewart, pauses to gaze at a daguerreotype of his intended bride, Ada, as Baines stands by with the Maori, hovering in the background. Stewart tilts the frame of the image so that its glass encasing transforms to a mirror, and his gazing upon Ada thus transforms to a narcissistic act—somewhat nervous, self-conscious and critically self-regarding. Stewart uses this 'mirror' to comb his hair; meanwhile his Maori helpers wait upon his instructions as to whether to move on or rest. (In the screen play there is an analogous scene in which Maori take turns combing their hair in a tiny piece of shared mirror. Its retention in the movie would perhaps have implied a universalism or solidarity, rather than a white man's lonely narcissism.) Yet Maori here are rendered as *mise en scène*, collectivised, blurred, shaded into a dark-continent background. As Dryburgh says of the landscape, 'We tried to represent it honestly, and let it be a dark place'.[25] One of the compelling debates on the movie centres on the fact that the anti-naturalistic apparatus of filters and the decision not to electrically light the 'dark' scenes enhances white skins to the point of luminosity and causes dark skins to be subordinated and

Maori as 'background' to the settler narrative.

vaguely erased. This contributes, it is argued, to an ideological code which is a kind of celebration of 'whiteness'. In this reading it is the bright and individualised settlers who claim the audiences' attention and affection; the Maori are without narrative or visual authority and merely support the exemplified white settler romance.[26] Dryburgh says he saw his mode as one which works to recreate a kind of antique visual style, rather than having an ideological dimension. For him it was 'a nineteenth century colour stills process, the autochrome, that inspired the unusual cinematography'.[27] That's why, he continues, 'we've tended to use strong colour accents in different parts of the film, drawing out the blue-green of the bush and the amber-rich mud.'[28] bell hooks and Leonie Pihama have criticised the movie as providing

> a series of constructions of Maori that are located firmly in the colonial gaze. These constructions range from the 'happy-go-lucky native' to the sexualised Maori women available at all times to service Pakeha men.'[29]

These are important criticisms since with any 'historical' drama there is an ethical challenge to the filmmakers to assess the degree to which representations might perpetuate neo-colonial thinking.

Yet the issue of racial representation is perhaps more ambivalent, and indeed contradictory. There are also significant forms of assertion, wit and resistant autonomy attributed to the Maori in *The Piano*. In the scene following the hair combing, Stewart and his party arrive at the beach to collect Ada and Flora, and their possessions (already to some extent claimed by the supernaturalised ocean). Filmed in discontinuous light on the beach, the Maori both mimic and mock Stewart and Ada. They flutter their hands in a play of faux sign language, they jest at Stewart's potency

('Watch it, old dry balls is getting touchy') and they lark around, signifying a lack of concern with the 'property' that so governs the Pakeha colonists. They also seem to be active and lively, in marked contrast to the static and constrained physical postures of the settlers. Stewart, discomforted by the mimicry, ill-at-ease in meeting his bride, asserts his power by rejecting Ada's demands to bring her piano from the beach. It is left behind—possibly to be picked up later but Stewart gives Ada no reassurance and her dismay is evident. There is a sense here that Maori and women are jointly subordinated, controlled by a kind of casual, taken for granted despotism. Maori are clearly in the role of servants, but the focus of consciousness and concern is Ada. Throughout *The Piano* there are many shots simply of her face, reaction shots, point-of-view shots, but also those which crucially imply her thoughts, shots which seem to endow her with centrality and subjectivity. If Maori are the objects of oppression, she is the subject; the camera rests meditatively on her silent face, calling forth the audiences' primary attachment to her and her plight.

On the walk back through the forest a Maori woman takes Ada's scarf and shawl and adorns herself: this is an unusual moment of appropriation from the 'other' side. In this movie possession, trading, and property are paramount: Maori are to some extent acculturated, dressed in European clothes, involved in bartering land for muskets and blankets, but they also retain their own language and are clever and critical observers of European settlement. They do not speak the 'broken' English of the native American in so many Hollywood westerns: they speak within the *mana* (power, prestige) of their own language (*Te Reo Maori*), translated into subtitles or verbalised by the alternative colonist, Baines.[30] On the return journey back from the beach to Stewart's homestead, the

Maori party carrying Ada and Flora's boxes of possessions is halted because they come to an area of land that is *tapu*—sacred and linked to prohibition. (In the screenplay the prohibition is more explicit: a Maori man says: 'Old man Pitama died here (points to the spot). The tapu hasn't been lifted.' And then: 'Go easy, there's a ghost down there!'[31]) Retaining a sacramental view of land and space, this small moment reminds us of the contradictions of colonised experience. Trading and loss of land coexist with a conviction of its essential indigenous power and of presence that remains invisibly forceful and active beyond the visible white tracks. In a later scene, Maori are depicted in the act of bartering their land. They refuse blankets then are shown muskets as an inducement to trade. Stewart's response, later on, is his irritable outburst to Baines: 'What do they want it for? They don't cultivate it, burn it back, anything. How do they even know its theirs?...' This exchange takes place alongside a row of white fence posts trailing

Baines: both the in-between and the go-between figure.

up a hill, a motif that elsewhere recurs as the mark of colonised space. It confirms Maori allegiance to an 'invisible' regime of value and also condemns Stewart's cultural misunderstanding and ignorance. The muskets are the symbol of cultural depredation, of foreign possessions, and of the dreadful threat to Maori culture of European weaponry.

The in-between and go-between figure here is Baines. Bearing the *moko* (tattoo) of traditional Maori culture, he is fluent in their language and apparently enjoys Maori respect. It's been suggested that this intermediate cultural positioning constructs a 'fantasy of reconciliation' between whites and Maori, a kind of allaying of postcolonial anxieties by permitting an imagined harmony of settler and indigenous ways of being.[32] In as much as this might be a restaging of colonial encounters, so that, for example, Baines seems separated out from the musket trade but is only depicted trading with Ada and Stewart, it is worth looking in detail at three inter-cultural scenes involving Maori.

In my first example, Baines is washing clothes in a river-hole and the subject of steady banter and interrogation by Maori men and women. It is a calm, almost utopian, scene of colonial contact. Baines is washing his clothes, squatting in the shallows, and the Maori community are sitting on branches of trees overhanging the water, looking down upon him. The encounter is relaxed, jolly; he is a kind of *assimilated* white man. The older woman, Hira (Tungia Baker), is teasing Baines about his lack of a sexual partner: 'You need a wife. It's no good having it sulk between your legs for the rest of your life.' Baines reveals he has a wife, one with 'a life of her own' back in England. A second reference is made to Baines's genitals and this is reinforced by another male character, Tahu (Neil Mika Gudsell), making a gesture of sexual invitation. A few children, mostly naked, are present during this exchange, taking place, significantly, both on and in water. In a movie about repression, sexual trading and the gradual discovery of reciprocated desire, Maori are represented as sexually emancipated and physically open. Traditionally, Maori were polygamous, did not value virginity and their language profoundly links the body and the social unit. (The word for tribe, *hapu*, is also that for 'pregnancy'; the word for a larger tribal group, *iwi*, also means 'bones'.) It is a feature of colonial discourse to sexualise the colonised—often a mechanism for suggesting their primitive barbarity. Here, however, sexual openness is valued, explicit and seen as a form of play. Baines and Ada are linked by having a sexual history; by contrast the mission house scenes between Stewart, Morag and Nessie, in which scandalised gossip, cups of tea and pursed-lip decorum governs, counterpoint Baines's relaxed, informal out-of-doors socialising. In one scene in the mission house two Maori girls, Heni (Carla Rupuha) and

Hira: a figure of authority

Mere (Mahina Tunui), one bearing *moko*, sing the white mans' anthem while they produce needle-work:

> *Got safe ah gayshy Quin*
> *Long lif a gashy Quin*
> *Got shayf a Quin*
> *Shendah Wikitoria*
> *Har-py en Clohria*
> *Long to rain ourush*
> *Got Safe ah Quin.*[33]

The girls sit sewing on the floor, signifying their servant status. But the parodic effect of their singing is to depreciate both the British monarchy and Christian authority. This is a very politicised script and the critique of colonial ideology seems direct and clear, so too is its criticism of missionary colonisation. In the screenplay the exchange between Baines and Hira at the riverhole goes thus:

> HIRA: I got the good wife for you Peini. She pray good. Clean.
> Read Bible. You sleep her Peini. She chief daughter.
> BAINES: No, no Bible readers.

Tahu ends his sexual innuendo by saying '*Hallelujah!*' implying an irreverent and witty misuse of religious language.[34] Protestant Christianity was remarkably successful in the European colonisation of New Zealand; yet the dominance of sexual discourse and the persistence of Maori social codes indicates the fundamental assertion of, and pride in, indigenous values. It suggests that an erotics of authenticity, and an authentic erotics—problematic notions, certainly—are both established as the standard of value for the text.

Colonial culture may also be read as invested in, and necessitating, the public performance of certain roles, rituals and indices of power. In the only European 'social' event of the movie, Ada accompanies Stewart to a community theatrical night in the school hall. One senses this is their first outing together as a couple: they are performing the roles of husband and wife, each dressed up, smiling stiffly, aware of their newly-attained social presence. In the audience is a mixture of Maori and Pakeha and on the stage a group of small children, all white, perform dances and songs charmingly in the costume of angels. There is an orange, almost sepia, filter to the scene and an ambience of sentimental pleasure and conviviality. Included in the entertainment is a version of the play, *Bluebeard's Castle*, and its function in the movie is crucial in terms of foreshadowing, unveiling and moral action. More particularly, it gives poetic force to the idea of *the screen*, the *staging* of vision and the anomalous combination of immersion and distance that constitutes cinema viewing. Screens exist everywhere in *The Piano*: fingers, curtains, petticoats, rain; all dematerialise the body into visions and shadows and reveal the *filmy* quality of the real recomposed by light. Campion's distinctive interest in emphatic composition of the shot, so evident in her early movies like the short, *Passionless Moments* (1983) and her first full length feature, *Sweetie* (1989), is transformed here to a preoccupation with mediated address and highly artificed communication.

A 1697 fairytale by Charles Perrault, *Bluebeard's Castle* is the exemplar of male, indeed marital, tyranny. Bluebeard marries and murders six wives, first entrusting each with a key and warning them not to enter a particular room (that which contains the other murdered wives). Each disobeys and is killed. The seventh wife discovers the bloody contents of the room, but escapes with the help of her brothers, who kill the tyrant. A narrative of possessive and violent marriage, it also privileges the 'key' as a symbol of unlocked desire and the inauguration of betrayal and violent revenge. Angela Carter's short story, *The Bloody Chamber*, may also be a reference here: in her version, the seventh wife's mother is the rescuer and in what is regarded as a classically feminist revaluing of female disobedience, Bluebeard is vanquished:

> The puppet master, open-mouthed, wide-eyed, impotent at the last, saw his dolls break free of their strings, abandon the rituals he had ordained for them since time began and start to live for themselves.[35]

This emphasises the degree to which the defeat of the husband, whom Carter casts as a puppet master, is also an unveiling of the masquerade of masculinity: Bluebeard's power as a master is overturned by the joint action of the mother and daughter.

In *The Piano* this drama is performed as an encrypted and dislocated sign—rather like *Hamlet*'s play within a play—by the character of Nessie. An awkward, large, somewhat infantilised woman, she is here seen moving with slow horror before a group of artistically 'severed' heads (women with their heads poked through bloody sheets) before she encounters Bluebeard in shadow-play, behind a screen. He is costumed as a grotesque, with a barrel belly, turban-like headwear and a large double-bladed axe. In shadow play, he threatens his seventh wife, who cowers before him. Yet the position of saviour is taken not by brothers (or a mother) but by Maori warriors seated with their chief in the audience. Apprehending the imminent violence they rise to their feet and act decisively by leaping towards the stage. As Bluebeard raises his axe and announces, 'Bare your neck!', they respond with the subtitled: 'Coward bite my club!... Let's see how it feels up your arse!'

The Maori tear away the screen and reveal Bluebeard affrighted in his cardboard armour. Chaos ensues and the 'decapitated'

'Bare your neck': the shadow play.

women on the stage scream. This commotion cuts abruptly to a quiet, composed shot, divided diagonally across the frame by the theatrical bed-sheet. Aunt Morag patiently explains the logic of theatre to the curious Maori: they are shown the mechanisms of the illusion and the resurrection, as it were, of the six dead wives. The oppressive confinement and control of women is corroborated even as it is uncovered as a staging.

In one reading it may be argued that this scene dishonours the Maori people by implying their ignorance, gullibility and inability to distinguish the real from the theatrical. They are apparently simple, innocent and unintelligent. Certainly there is no shortage of critics who consider the representation of Maori problematic, one suggesting, for example, that these are 'primitivist discourses which construct Maori as outside culture'.[36] But another way of viewing this scene—and it is the one I strongly favour—is that Maori here are shown as motivated by intrinsically honourable and noble aims. There is no reason why they should understand the conventions and tricks of an unfamiliar representational form (pantomime and shadow play and—implicitly—the filmic illusion of reality). They are nevertheless given spontaneously to ethical action and intervention on behalf of a threatened woman. They participate, one might say, in an implicit critique of the misogyny of a white masculinist culture that treats the slaying of a woman as entertainment. Moreover they are symbolically allied with the cause of women against serial and pathological brutality. The *Bluebeard* episode radically foreshadows the abuse that Ada will suffer—in keeping with the wave-like return of tropes and symbols that structure the poetics of the movie—and it also presages the eventual liberation of the wife.

This shadowing device also references the archival foundations of cinema, recalling the tale of the Lumière brothers' first public screening in 1895 of a train arriving at the station at La Ciotat, during which viewers, misunderstanding the vision on the screen, allegedly called out in alarm and ducked beneath their seats. Campion often addresses the fact that cinema is a combination of light and shadow and the magnified projection of shapes. She is interested in illusionism, gauzy radiance and the willing suspension of disbelief, and tends to draw attention to the fact that cinema involves a seancing of entities 'not-there'. In Campion's film *Holy Smoke* (1999), for example, the issue of cultural difference is crucially represented by moments of abstraction. Ruth (Kate Winslett) is an Australian woman from Sydney 'seduced' into an Indian cult, and her loss of self-possession and delusion are reflected in a canny play of visual styles. There is a gaudy desert

THE PIANO

sky, the lurid palette of hippiedom, an apotheosis (in which the heroine is envisioned floating in the sky as a Hindu goddess) rendered in a kitschy kaleidoscope. These are the tokens of bold and inventive filmmaking, reminding us that cinema can *show* what we like to keep private, inflate into images what might seem otherwise inexpressible. Campion has always been interested in the incommensurable, in ideas and things not fitting together, and it is a feature of her style to work this out visually, as well as conceptually. She is interested, too, in knowing and misknowing—words are treacherous and confounding; the shape of the body, by contrast, is a kind of direct apprehension, an iconic sign, even if artificial and ultimately phantasmagoric.

5

HUSH-HUSH-HUSH: SILENCE, WORDS, MUSIC

Campion's biopic of Janet Frame, *An Angel at My Table*, ends with an act of serene artistic creation. She depicts Frame working on a manuscript in a caravan, late at night, and in a mood of pleasurable achievement reads (in voice-over) her final lines: 'Hush-hush-hush, the grass, and the wind, and the fir, and the sea are saying: hush-hush-hush.'[37]

This wholly lovely ending affirms a connection between silence and creativity, and indeed affirms the paradoxical 'wording' of silence. In a gentle wave motion, and ending with 'the sea', quiet settles gradually across the natural world. Traditionally regarded as disempowerment, silence in this gesture is a form of completion, satisfaction and individual assertion, an inverted speaking into a disembodied voice-over. In a famously influential argument, film theorist Kaja Silverman contends that the separation of voice and body for the female subject in cinema works for proto-feminist ends, making her 'inaccessible to definitive male interpretation'.[38] She is evasive, rather than lacking presence, elusive rather than merely lost. Ada is not *simply* silent; her opening voice-over suggests instead that profound strategies of displacement and 'signing' are at work.

THE PIANO

How might a movie represent a silent heroine? If the silence has the same nonsensical quality of existing in the utterance the word 'hush', then there is similarly a scepticism concerning the status of language and speech at the heart of *The Piano* and a systemic relocation, even alienation, of Ada's meaning. One of the principle sites of displacement is the daughter, Flora. Consider this exchange between Aunt Morag, Nessie and Flora:

> AUNT MORAG: I can't imagine a fate worse than being dumb.
>
> NESSIE: To be deaf.
>
> AUNT MORAG: Oh, ay, to be deaf too. Terrible. Awful.
>
> FLORA: Actually, to tell you the whole truth, Mother says most people speak rubbish, and it's not worth a listen.
>
> AUNT MORAG: Well, that 'tis a strong opinion.
>
> FLORA: Ay, it's unholy.

In this scene Nessie and Morag are costuming Flora as an angel for a play, yet her conversation is anything but angelically innocent. Aware of the complicated status of her mother's 'disability', Flora is 'voicing' her mother's contempt for everyday speech, and also suggesting, possibly strategically, her own split allegiance between forces of orthodoxy and dissent.

It is given to Flora to translate her mother's signing into speech, and as such she offers in a girl-voice Ada's adult opinions. This practiced conflation of consciousness will lead her to betray her mother, ironically as she tries to assert her autonomy. It will also sexualise the daughter and emerge in her terrible outburst, characterised by obscenities:

> FLORA: I shan't practice and I don't care. Blast and damn and bugger her! Bloody, bloody bugger her! Let her fall face down in the boiling bloody mud! Let a spitting mad dog bite her till she bleeds.

The displaced voice.

Still wearing her angel wings some time after the theatrical event, Flora expresses a fierce verbal violence towards her mother who has just gone voluntarily to see her lover Baines after he has returned her piano. It is the culmination of a series of exclusions from Ada's company and the point at which, perhaps, Flora realises she has lost her mother's ardent attention. In a miasmic, smoky blue forest, Stewart comes upon Flora's outburst:

>STEWART: Where's your mother? Where's she gone?
>FLORA: To Hell!

Flora screams directly at the camera, as though cursing her mother. Her fists are clenched, her expression is furious, her whole body is rigid and trembling with rage. It is a shocking scene not just because it encapsulates Flora's anger—a tantrum might plausibly be the consequence of her mother's rejection—but because the fury contained within the shouted words reveals the dangerous crisis of language and the imminent possibility of violation of the body. Misaligned voices and words, the eruption of curses, the wounding capacity of thwarted desire; these are all present in this unholy and matricidal speech. Flora's role in voicing her mother collapses at this point: language is trespass against the inner world and the privacy of sexual congress; it brings into the explicit and obscene realm what should remain hidden. Perhaps, too, there is a suggestion of the strain of silence for the child of a mute mother: in the end it is intolerable since it fixes the daughter in an echoing function and erodes her own distinctive self.[39]

The central object of displaced voice, however, is of course the piano. A prosthetic of identity and self, it stands in for and supplements Ada's voice, implying that which somehow directly expresses her character. It also reveals territories of extra-linguistic and possibly pre-linguistic meaning: feeling, passion, dream state, imagination. Prosthetic augmentation of the self, according to feminist philosopher Elizabeth Grosz, is by no means unusual or exceptional, but is our constant state of relation to both organic and inorganic matter, the basis of our 'most elaborate reflection and invention'.[40] In an important development in rethinking the relation of culture and biology, Grosz finds the creative capacities of identity as in part the adaptation and fabrication of ourselves in relation to the stimulating 'things' at our disposal. Yet Ada is clearly atypical in the degree to which she has given over the performance of her 'self' to an inanimate object, and the 'original' compositions that carry and regulate her personal meaning. (There are one or two occasions in which Ada plays Scottish folk tunes, teaching Flora, or a clunky Chopin waltz, rebuking Baines; but in most cases her score is Nyman's and this registers her modernity and mis-fit with her culture.)

Ada is an enigma to the community she has joined. When Aunt Morag is trying to decipher the riddle of Ada, she comments:

> It's hopeless. You know I am thinking of the piano. She does not play the piano as we do, Nessie ... No, she is a strange creature. And her playing is strange, like a mood that passes into you ... Now your playing is plain and true, and that is what I like. To have a sound creep inside you is not at all pleasant.

This speech is made within a screen, as it were. Aunt Morag is urinating in the bush and her two Maori maids and Nessie hold up a blanket to give her privacy. The blanket keeps slackening and Aunt Morag commands 'Up! Up!' This scene ends with birds fluttering unseen in the bushes nearby: Nessie and the girls leap away, shrieking, and Morag is left to hastily kick over her leavings. Repression is a crucial element in Campion's logic here. The screening of bodily functions, ludicrously excessive and unnecessary, equate to a dismissal of Ada's music. It is an almost schematic aligning of repression with a certain kind of conventional sound and the will to control. The flutter of birds that disturbs the party is 'natural' sound, intruding to remind the viewer of all that is uncontrollable, indigenous, and outside social decorum.

The *sound that creeps inside you* is, of course, the music of composer Michael Nyman, but intended to suggest Ada's own repertoire, as if, almost by instinct 'she had been the composer'.[41] As Claudia Gorbman, in a wonderful article on the movie's music, states:

> Through the music's repetition and almost constantly arpeggiated chords, we get the impression that the music is *personal*, music created by Ada over hundreds of hours of playing. She never plays from published sheet music, but from 'inside her head'.[42]

Certainly Ada plays in a self-enclosed, private way, closing her eyes at points of rhapsodic engagement, seeming to enact a kind

THE PIANO

of tonal and melodic identification. The signature tune, 'The Heart Asks Pleasure First', is a swelling, rolling, catchy piece, anachronistically modern in its form. The word 'pleasure' is significant: the first scene of Ada playing in New Zealand, when the piano is still on the beach encased in its packing, shows Ada's hands entering the slot of a pulled-away board and pleasurably fingering the exposed keys. As she enters the music, she is self-pleasuring, in a way; the eroticising of the piano is established early in this movie. Watching the act on a second occasion is Baines, who has consented after badgering to lead Flora and Ada down to the beach to visit their stranded piano, and his bewildered response is important. Baines is seduced by the exaltation and pleasure he witnesses, and by the glimpse of Ada's sexualised touch. He is here the desiring subject, walking in circles around the performer, who is essentially oblivious to his stalking presence.

What follows is a sexual and trading narrative based around six piano 'lessons'. In exchange for 80 acres of land, Stewart has traded the piano to Baines without Ada's consent. In order to gain access to her piano and 'earn' it back, Ada agrees to 'teach' Baines with private lessons in his hut. He announces ominously: 'You see, I'd like us to make a deal. There's things I want to do while you play. If you let me, you can earn it back.' Although Ada is not 'wordless'—since she writes messages on a pad hung around her neck—Baines is illiterate, so that all communication between them must be by the languages of the body and of music. Baines 'just wants to listen'; he has no technical interest in the mastery of the piano; rather, he wishes to see, touch, smell and hear Ada's presence, or, as the critic Sue Gillett astutely points out, he

> jealously wishes to be the piano, to be the receiver of such rapturous touching ... to have such haunting music evoked

> in and through his own body, to tremble under the powerful
> cadences of [Ada's] transcendence ... [43]

Investment in the piano is in a substitute body, or, in another sense, an extended body—for both Baines and Ada. Later, Stewart learns what these so called 'lessons' really involve and attempts to rape Ada. In an inter-cut the piano is shown being crudely banged upon by Maori, a rather obvious and racially insensitive metaphor for misunderstanding how to touch the instrument. By contrast, when Baines is alone with the piano, he encircles it, naked, as though in an act of private devotion. He wipes its surfaces, leans towards and over it, finds in himself a tenderness and regard that will transform his trading relationship with Ada.

The music soundtrack to *The Piano* follows the developing erotic relationship, starting with Ada playing music with titles like 'Silver Fling' (played at the first lesson), followed by 'Big My Secret' (the second) and 'The Attraction of the Pedalling Ankle' (the third). With each lesson, the music reflects the way in which Baines raises the sexual stakes. Each time, Ada has to remove one more article of clothing and allow Baines greater access to her body. When Ada begins to reciprocate Baines's feelings of attraction, the music, 'A Bed of Fern', shifts to the non-diegetic, detached from her on-screen action to signify the way desire now exceeds objects and spaces. When Stewart uses his axe to amputate Ada's finger, the scene is 'played' to the score of 'A Sacrifice'.[44] Ada may not speak, but the soundtrack is eloquent in her stead. Rarely has a movie given such prominence to the function sound plays in the meaning of a film, or to the symbolic locations and uses of a body-self substitute in this way. The silence then is therefore necessarily ironic: Ada gestures, stares, acts in social presence, and never attempts to utter a single syllable; but,

THE PIANO

of course, as her prefacing voice-over insists: *I don't think of myself as silent.*

Another dimension of the silence is Ada's signing to Flora. In beautifully intimate scenes, often on or in bed and enwreathed in a burnishing orange glow, Ada 'speaks' to her daughter with her sinuously expressive hands. The subtitled translation accords with Maori representation on the screen: spoken English is just one of many forms of communication in the movie and not at all associated with inner life or centres of value. Here is Ada, her face close in a lover's propinquity to her daughter, telling a fragment of the 'back-story' of her life:

A piano lesson.

    ADA: I've told you this story many times.
    FLORA: Tell me again. Was he your teacher?
    ADA: Yes. I could lay my thoughts out before him like a sheet.
    FLORA: Why didn't you get married?
    ADA: He became frightened and stopped listening.

Ada's gesture of the laying down of thoughts—her hands sweep and flutter, she arches her neck—appears dance-like; it expresses the body's telling capacities and implies that Flora knows of her own illegitimacy and her mother's former relationship. Subtle though this knowledge is, it is contained in the movements of hands without any suggestion of lack or loss. The relinquishment is the teacher's, not Ada's and listening, rather than speaking, is given prestige in interpersonal relationships. A further sign encounter goes like this:

>ADA: And the wind said, 'Remember how we used to play?'
>Then the wind took her hand and said, 'Come with me'.
>But she refused.
>FLORA: I won't call him Papa. I won't even look at him.

This episode takes place before Ada and Flora have met Stewart and sets up a resistance, from the outset, to the new family structure. Yet it is a highly lyrical fragment, and sign language here is the capacious repository of story, of the magical and the 'play' of ideas. Significantly, too, it obliquely metaphorises the social, or in any case leads Flora to reassert her allegiance to her mother. It should be added that the folktale and mystical quality of this story extends to the playing of the piano. In an extraordinary short scene much later in the movie, Ada plays the piano in her sleep. Her long dark hair is loose, she is rigid, transfixed, and with open glassy eyes stares unseeing into the night's distance. Stewart holds up a lamp to illuminate Ada's face and Flora explains to him that when her mother was a girl she sleepwalked away from her father's house, travelling so far barefoot that her feet became torn and bloody. Playing the piano therefore extends into the unconscious realm, and again weds the child and the mother in a collapse in time. Stewart looks horrified and taken aback at this intelligence, yet it confirms that Ada is indeed an exceptional woman—troubled, passionate, given to wild inner excursions.

6
EROTICS, FEELING AND THE MASCULINE

As if Stewart's conversion of the daguerreotype to a mirror wasn't warning enough, the details and circumstances of Ada's 'wedding' portend her failed relationship with him. 'If there cannot be a ceremony, there can at least be a photograph', announces Aunt Morag, as Ada is dressed in her wedding gown. At the start of the scene the gown is shown worn by the comical reverend minister, in a kind of cross-dressing trope of masculine insecurity for which Campion is celebrated. The dress is, as one critic reminds us, a mere 'photographer's prop', a false over-garment, a symbol of the displacement of real feeling and genuine ceremony by an act of convenient, sham representation.[45]

In a film preoccupied with forms of *masquerade*, with costumes, bonnets, hooped crinoline skirts, and with, moreover, acts of gradual disrobing, the emphasis on counterfeit costume, merely for show, carries a strong ideological force. Campion is a filmmaker highly aware of the link between cross-dressing and the investigation of gender roles. The production diary of Claire Corbett, an assistant editor of the movie, contains this entry:

> Photographs from the shoot in New Zealand line the walls of the cutting rooms: photos of the actors in costume, of the crew, of Harvey Keitel in a dress. Jane Campion always had a dress day at least once during her shoots; all the cast and crew have to wear dresses. The men love it. The most macho change their dresses several times a day. Often the women find it more traumatic. Jane says she feels much closer to her male crew once she's seen them in a dress.[46]

The masquerade of gender is a persistent concern in Campion's movies; she often investigates the social dimension of costuming and its forms of value.

Implausibly, the wedding photograph is taken in the drenching rain. Ada sits under a parasol on what appears to be a miniature stage, and in a remarkable shot we see Stewart's scrutinising eye in a monstrous close-up, looking through the camera. This is almost a cliché of the controlling masculine gaze; yet in other ways this scene has a compelling absurdism and is artfully succinct in its suggestion of misconnection and estrangement. Seated together, Stewart takes out a small comb and with ridiculous care tidies his wet, greasy hair, suggesting a kind of neurotic insecurity beneath his power; Ada stares blankly ahead, awash in blue-tinted gloom. After the photograph Ada hastily retreats, ripping the lace of the wedding dress as she tears it from her everyday clothes, and in a moment indicative of extreme isolation, stands gazing dejectedly through the screen of a watery window pane, imagining her beached piano. The 'wedding', such as it is, is devoid of loving feeling between Ada and Stewart; in its place is a longing for the lost object of desire.

The rhythm of these two scenes, or rather the shift between them, is restrained but moving. There is no dialogue from Stewart, no words of marital affection. Instead, Ada's silence here, standing

THE PIANO

Stewart: banal literalist and possessive materialist.

alone at the window, is a state of bereft, anguished loss. Her signature tune rises extradiegetically and the camera cuts back to the beach to locate the stranded piano, awash and imperilled in the high-tidal shallows. Affect in cinema, the emotional response of audiences to the moods and emotions on screen is sometimes simply a matter of the length of a single shot. Forms of empathetic 'contagion' and 'affective mimicry' often require a certain kind of pause on the face. Carl Plantinga argues that it is the extended resting of the camera on Ada's melancholy face that in scenes like this one signify and arouse an intensified response.[47] Conventionally, in mainstream cinema, a face shot is on average about six seconds long; here and elsewhere they extend to thirty-three. In addition to this concentration on Ada as the 'subject' of the movie, the filming also implies a kind of transcendental subject, an emancipated point of view shot, skimming from the sky to find the subject of desire. (This cinematic glissade will recur later on in a Hitchcockian tribute, zooming, *Vertigo*-like, into Ada's coiled hairstyle, the camera—and the score—lift to slide across the forest, signifying her searching desire for Baines. Not a point of view shot in any usual sense, its 'de-realising ethereality' nevertheless suggests a flying consciousness, a supernatural vision, and is the mark of the 'romantic' that possibly genders responses to the movie.[48])

Stewart is a bluff, pragmatic character, stiff with unacknowledged feeling and awkward hesitation. Although mostly depicted performing 'manly' pursuits—wood-chopping, in particular—he is unmanned by Ada's silence and non-compliance. Indeed it is the shifts in Stewart's character, as much as the romance between Ada and Baines, that construct the narrative trajectory of the movie. He is also, in a peculiar way, a kind of innocent. Jane Campion

THE PIANO

imagined a nineteenth-century limit, in terms of sexual knowledge and the formation of character:

> They have nothing to prepare themselves for its strength and power. We grew up with all those magazines of courtship, giving us lots of little rules and ways of handling it. We grew up with so many expectations around it, that it's almost like the pure sexual erotic impulse is lost to us. But for them ... the husband Stewart had probably never had sex at all. So for him the experience of sex or feelings of sexual jealousy, would have been personality-transforming.[49]

The parodic wedding photograph scene confirms the movie's critique of bourgeois (or arranged) marriage. As in *The Portrait of a Lady*, marriage is exposed as a social contract based on impure motive and the disadvantage of the woman. In the screenplay of *The Piano*, the following lines are given to a blind piano tuner whom Baines thoughtfully enlists to repair the piano before his 'lessons':

> My wife sang with a clear bell tone. After we were married she said she didn't feel like singing, that life made her sad. And that's how she lived, lips clamped closed over a perfect voice, a beautiful voice.[50]

Here, even an apparently beneficent figure acknowledges by implication the losses and compromises of marriage, and adds a parallel example of the silenced wife.

When Stewart trades Ada's piano to Baines in exchange for land, he has no idea of the symbolic mutilation he is enacting. Just as he cannot understand the Maori relationship to land (*How do they even know it's theirs?*) he is a banal literalist and a possessive materialist, seeing value principally in objects and their accumulation. This is emphasised when, having discovered Ada and Baines' relationship, Stewart literally imprisons her in his house, boarding up windows and attaching locks to the outside of the doors. There is a tiny scene in which Stewart, hearing Ada and Flora giggle and play in an adjacent room, flicks distractedly through a scrapbook of botanical specimens. It is a neat symbol of the morbid and desiccating capture of nature, of containment, ordering and categorisation. Associated with the colonial enterprise of cutting down trees (New Zealand kauri timber was a principal colonial export), Stewart is, unsurprisingly, the figure of the cuckold in keeping with the Romantic equations of the narrative (nature-sexuality-feeling). He twice attempts to rape Ada—once as she returns from making love to Baines, chasing her through the forest, moving with submarine impediment and slow motion expression; a second time when she is lying unconscious after he has attacked her with an axe. Aroused by Ada's passivity, Stewart begins fondling her thigh and unbuckling his trousers, only to be stopped when she opens her eyes and fixes him with an unblinking accusation. Stewart halts, ashamed. His is a sexuality that requires a wife's submission, not contestation, and certainly not *her* desire.

In one of the most audacious and unexpected scenes in the movie—one bathed, once again, in the sensuous orange filter—Ada comes to Stewart at night and begins slowly to touch his prone, half-asleep body. Pulling back his trousers, she strokes his buttocks and inserts her hand between his thighs. It is a dreamy scene, full of gentle possibility. Ada is attempting in a sense to offer Stewart a lesson in responsiveness, an erotics of silence and the pleasure of investigative touch. But Stewart recoils, his expression one of confusion and disgust. It is a moment in which their relationship might have been reconstructed, but the sexual agency of the heroine meets no understanding. Occurring during her 'imprisonment', Ada is indicating her knowledge of another kind of liberation.

Many of the debates on *The Piano* centre precisely on its depiction of heterosexual romance and its ambivalence in relation to male and female sexuality. The controversy turns on Baines's initiation of his relationship with Ada—in collusion with Stewart—through the market system of economic possession, domination and trade. Baines has no interest in 'learning' the piano; what he wants initially is to exploit Ada's longing for repossession of her instrument, in order to extract sexual favours. Confirming the logic of exploitation and profit at the base of the colonial encounter, Baines offers to 'trade back' the piano, key by key, in return for forms of sexual access. Ada's response to this challenge is both acquiescent and defiant: she insists on shifting the currency to black keys (which, of course, are fewer) and this signals her own awareness of the grounds of negotiation, her compromise of selfhood by entering into the bargain, and also the high personal value she attaches to the piano. Since the movie has already depicted Ada's dependence on her piano, her tearful agreement to the trade establishes Baines as a dominating and manipulative man, corrupted by the sexual and economic power of his situation.

Yet Baines's behaviour is a slow, one might say strategically and seductively slow (both in terms of his intentions and the sexual tension in the movie), escalation of physical contact. Baines circles quietly behind Ada as she plays her piano, reaching forward now and then to touch her, commanding her, by stages, to remove one more garment, making his presence felt as an intervention between the woman and her prosthetic self. At one point he lies on the floor beneath the piano, and fingers Ada through a discovered hole in her black worsted stocking. 'Higher! Higher!' Baines instructs, requiring Ada to lift her hooped skirt—bizarrely echoing but inverting the *Up! Up!* of Aunt Morag's neurotic covering-over—and the veiling/unveiling motif is again invoked. The movie relies fundamentally on close-ups of hands, and this scene, much discussed in writings on *The Piano*, seems to have a particularly captivating force.[51] Dana Polan argues,

> no image perhaps incarnates for many spectators the affective eroticism of *The Piano* more than an extreme close-up of Baines's finger lightly passing through a small tear in Ada's clothes to touch her flesh with a caress that is simultaneously timid and bold.[52]

Recalling Vivien Sobchack's 'cinesthesia', we can acknowledge here the erotic charge of so focussed (and metonymic) a gesture. 'The erotic', as Roland Barthes says, 'is where the garment gapes'.[53] In this case fleshly access, in so restrictive a scenario, is heightened in its evocative and provocative power, and works suggestively, in the manner of Victorian fiction, to provide an emblem of the tactility of female pleasuring. In another sequence Baines, eyes closed, deeply inhales the scent of Ada's jacket. He is linked not to the gaze but to a broader range of sensuous apprehension: to touching, smell and hearing. The blind piano tuner, it must be noted, sniffs the piano—'scent', he proclaims, 'and salt of course'.

In some accounts this is a relationship premised on the ratification and aestheticisation of rape. Ada learns to love her harasser and embodies women's powerlessness and the pernicious idea that women wish to be dominated. In contending accounts, Ada learns her own agency, become self-assertive and identifies, above all, the primacy of her own desire.[54] Campion is also charged with misogyny, or with constructing a feminist heroine. What these debates reveal is the complication and heterodoxy of the sexual scenes, and perhaps an inclination to the themes of female masochism which seem so evident in her later feature film, *In the Cut* (2003).

It is important, in either case, to acknowledge the point at which the trading relationship is annulled by Baines. I would argue there is a crucial 'revaluation of value' operating to shift the premise of the lovers' engagement. Although he has reached the point of persuading Ada to lie chastely naked beside him, Baines realises that the relationship he wants with Ada exceeds the logic of trade. He tells her: 'I am giving you back the piano. I have had enough. The arrangement is making you a whore and me wretched. I want you to care for me. But you can't.'

Releasing Ada from the obligation to be touched, Baines returns, inadvertently, her own self-possession, so that the relationship now has the possibility of reciprocated desire. The trade and property relationship has been overturned by the *gift* relationship: in the economy of the gift Ada is able to realise her own desire for Baines and to participate, of her own free will, in their erotic connection. During the period of the piano lessons, the effect of the encounters has not been to cement Baines's masculine power. Curiously, it is he who has become sexualised, dependant and weak. In a remarkable scene he presents himself naked to Ada; it is a moment which exposes male nudity as an object for the female gaze and establishes 'an equal state of undress'.[55] Campion is credited with refusing typical Hollywood conventions of nudity and finding an aesthetic that shows Baines's 'body [as] strong but vulnerable, sexual, but not idealised'.[56] Significantly, too, Baines is feminised during his 'lessons'. The scene in which he announces his abjection—his *own* disempowerment—is that which compels Ada to come to him. His longest speech in the movie goes like this:

> Ada, Ada. I am unhappy. Because I want you. Because my mind has seized on you and can think of nothing else. This is why I suffer. I am sick with longing. I don't eat. I don't sleep so if you've come with no feeling for me ... then go. Go. Go! Get out! Leave!

Baines is sitting in the smoky chamber of his hut, his head drooping down, his demeanour miserable. He moves to open the door to encourage Ada to leave and she slaps him about the face before subsiding into the icon of romance, the on-screen kiss. They kiss 'with enormous succulence and great deliberation', as Virginia Woolf says of Anna and Vronsky in her account of a silent film of *Anna Karenina*.[57] Romance is achieved. The luscious tension is dispersed. There is a sinking to the floor—in a movie replete with the spatial dynamics of risings and sinkings. But the representation of sexual congress that follows is highly unusual. Typically, one knows to the point of exhaustion the tedious repertoire of cinematic sex: throbbing thighs, gasping women, Vaseline smeared fantasy, a head thrown back in clichéd ecstasy. In Campion's version—and I believe it to be a then unprecedented moment in popular cinema—the woman is pleasured first.[58] Baines opens Ada's jacket, but instead of the usual, familiar codes of ravishment, dives beneath her hooped skirt to give oral pleasure. Both private and explicit, it legitimates and affirms female sexual desire. Ada is standing, half clothed; Baines is beneath her, hidden. The shot of the lovers naked together is also oddly both private and explicit. They appear fleshly and firm; they embrace heartily but without the inhuman gloss and blur of cinematic convention. With a mid-distance decorum, the lovemaking is filmed framed between the red cloth curtains—an opened screen—of Baines's bed. It is restrained filming, with Baines's body shielding Ada's, enclosing her in the colour-coded ambience of their intimacy.

Watching their illicit union is Stewart. Already established as a voyeur, not least in the magnified authority of his eye in the camera, here he stands in ironically for the position of the male spectator. Stewart spies at the lovers through the wooden slats of Baines's hut, and is unable to pull himself away. His dog companion licks his hand in a somewhat crass analogy to the cunnilingus he is witnessing, and Stewart wipes the dog's saliva on the wooden wall of the house. This moment depletes our sympathy; it renders him foolish. Passive, arrested, shocked and immobilised, Stewart is fascinated but impotent, mesmerised but unable to act or intervene. He later lies beneath the house to watch through the floorboards, and one of Ada's jacket buttons loosens as she dresses and rolls through the cracks to fall onto his neck. It is a metafilmic moment of unlikely pathos: something beyond the screen almost hits him in the eye, something that ought to be beyond vision is materialised, and the audience's sense of viewing positions—and of our own voyeurism—is suddenly made circumspect. The next shot is of Ada continuing to dress and Baines saying 'Wait. I don't know what you're thinking. Does this mean something to you? I already miss you. Ada, do you love me?' To which she replies by lifting his shirt and kissing the place of his heart. The interrogative is important. This is not a movie in which actors say '*I love you*' with the dull conclusiveness and assertion of romantic closure. Since Ada cannot speak, her declaration must be gestural and symbolic; similarly Baines is in the position of pleading for signs, of wishing for a voice that might confirm what the body already knows.

7

THE MUTILATION

There is a sense in which *The Piano* is a kind of trauma narrative. Characterised by wounding, forms of forgetting and loss, from the beginning there is a suggestion that Ada may have a traumatic past. The night-time sleep-walking/sleep-playing—which happens immediately after Stewart imprisons her—may signify some unspeakable and troubled response to her father since, according to Flora at least, in the childhood event she was walking away from her father's house, her feet bloody with the effort. It is difficult to know, since Flora is a fabulist, whether or not to credit this story, but it lies suggestively, like an informative trace, in the text, possibly lending a sinister dimension to Ada's elective mutism. The power of the father, or the patriarch, is in any case associated with wounding, not with care.

After the lovemaking scene, the spirited mood continues into play between mother and daughter. Flora and Ada are pirouetting in the bedroom, giggling, chasing each other with a hairbrush; something energetic has been released; there is a marvellous delight in the body and its interpersonal enjoyment. Stewart watches them together, tormented by his knowledge. And it is in the next scene, once again coded aquamarine, that Stewart tries to rape

Ada, seizing her, dragging her under, thrusting his arm aggressively beneath her skirt, resignified now as dangerously impeding and containing. The proximity of the consensual lovemaking and the molestation is shocking; Stewart is revealed as one who responds to sexual jealousy with physical attack. Significantly, he has very few lines in the script that are spoken to Ada. There is no 'voicing' of his unhappiness, his witness, his seething emotions; nor does he ask Ada to account for her adulterous behaviour. Ada's silence inhibits him, it further erodes his own expressive capacities and possibly too he does not assume her intelligence and full subjectivity; he cannot imagine her experience or point of view without the aid of words. The score of the attempted rape scene is pounding and disturbing; it is difficult to watch this visually and aurally stylised scene without the dread knowledge that rape is a treatment of the body as brute matter, a fundamental ignoring of the psychical interiority that allows others their precious humanity.[59] That it is filmed as a kind of nightmare—with nocturnal and watery tones, abnormal expressions, the strangely unreal, grasping undergrowth that makes the forest-scape scary, as though borrowed from fairytale or horror cinema—compounds the sense of both emotional distortion and physical entrapment. Only Flora's interruption, stumbling upon the scene having heard, with alarm, the discordant piano, saves Ada.

In the incarceration that follows, Ada turns inward. As Stewart nails and boards the house closed (with Flora's direction: 'Here, Papa!'), she behaves with solipsistic, abandoned self-regard, kissing her own image in the mirror, ignoring her daughter, giving way to the luxurious unhappiness of sexual longing. The piano is no longer a source of expression or existential surety; as Flora practices, Ada wanders away, self-enclosed, lonely. ('Now that she has it, why doesn't she play?' Stewart asks.) It is in this period that Ada sexually touches Stewart, seeming to transfer her knowledge of the body, if not her affections, and finds herself spurned by a panicking, inadequate substitute. She is libidinised, as it were; in every gesture there is a body-memory of what has passed between her and Baines, and it is, by implication, unforgettable. Authentic sexual pleasure is not, after all, a fleeting and circumstantial thing; it is a releasing of the self, a charged somatic awareness, carried beyond the bedroom, of the privileged humanity granted in loving exchange. The lover's body leaves an ineradicable imprint. It leaves the self co-responsively alert and invested in reconnecting.

Misunderstood by her husband, agonisingly lonely, it is in a sense no surprise when, after Stewart decides to 'trust' Ada by re-opening the house, that she seeks again, almost immediately, to contact Baines. Taking a key from her piano, Ada burns along its stem the inscription *Dear George, you have my heart, Ada*. This is a puzzling and complicated act. It is a form of self-mutilation, because the piano is disarticulated with one key missing, and because Baines cannot read, it seems a nonsense to write to him. It may simply be of the order of a continuity mistake (the director forgetting that the character Baines is illiterate), but a more interesting way of reading the act is as a compulsive repetition in a movie full of other wave-like repetitions and as another symbol of the fraught contest between words and images.[60] We see just a glimpse, in an earlier scene, of another inscribed key (a love-heart and a few letters are just visible)—Ada may be compulsively replaying her earlier lost romance with Flora's father; or she may be taking the active role, signalling her need to address her inamorata more specifically, in words as well as symbols. I've not seen any critical comment on the inscribing of the key, but it seems to me a declaration of compelling power. This is not Bluebeard's key, loaded with threat and fear, but it is a token of the body now incomplete, of what is touched now disconnected, of the wish to be re-integrated, or re-membered, by a lover's return. A slender, surprisingly beautiful object, it is also a body part, it is also Ada.

Flora is washing doll's clothes, playing mother, when Ada insists she deliver the piano key to Baines. In the screenplay the direction states:

> Under the sheets Flora has constructed a doll's clothes line on which she hangs small strips of cloth. Ada hands her the key wrapped and tied in white cotton. Ada signs. Her black shadow behind the sheet recalls the macabre play.[61]

Flora rebukes her mother with a stern tone: 'We're not supposed to visit him!' But Ada insists, and Flora is sent on her errand. When she chooses the right, rather than the left, fork in the trail, she betrays her mother by taking the key to Stewart, engaged in fencing land atop a picturesque hill, and there is a cleaving of the emotional territory of the movie. Stewart leaves the key behind (and in a repetition of an earlier scene his Maori workers are shown ignorantly striking it: 'See, it's lost its voice'), and Flora follows her enraged 'papa' back to the house.

In a brilliantly edited and realised scene, Ada is attacked. She is reading when Stewart arrives—quietly interiorised, sunk in words—and he raises his axe and chops with a loud vibrating thwack into the hood of her piano. In an eccentric image of disorder and the disruption of the domestic, a reel of cotton audibly unspools, toppling from the piano. Stewart seizes Ada, and pushes her roughly against the wall, then, retrieving the axe, brutally

The mutilated woman collapses.

drags her outside. Violence in cinema is often so extravagant as to prohibit all feeling; filmmakers rely on the body-count thrill of blown-away enemies, the spectacular collapse or explosion of bodies, the comic-book hyperbole of actions and larger-than-life sound effects. To recover the facticity of violence in its painful and visceral power is to make the severing of a single finger an utter catastrophe. Campion achieves this principally by slowing time and vision and recording with ghastly intimacy the soundtrack and close-up reaction shots. As Stewart mutilates his wife, we see the blue face of Ada register the act in stupefied pain, we see too her daughter's white face and dress spattered brightly with blood. Flora screams, and this triangulation of the moment towards the point of view of child witness is what contains and expresses the emotion of horror.

The next shots are startling. Filmed from behind, Ada lifts herself slowly, cradling her damaged hand close, and moves away, almost sliding, into the middle distance. The soundtrack is melancholy and slow, and the film registers the altered time of trauma, the sense of arrest, of dislocation, of out-of-synch response. Ada falls not with a dramatic hurl or a shrill plunging over, but simply *down*, seeming to be swallowed by her waterlogged skirt as she folds slowly into her pain. Rain is pouring in immersing sheets and the submarine self is again evoked. There is the close-miked sound of rainfall, Ada's breathing and even a gentle poof of air as she falls into her skirt.[62] There is nothing naturalistic about this scene, yet it is immediately affecting. When the 'real-time' again resumes, Stewart gives the severed finger to Flora with the message: 'Take this to Baines. Tell him if he tries to see her again I'll take another. And another.'

There exist a vast number of articles on *The Piano* that speak of Stewart's 'castration' of Ada in hacking off her finger. But this seems too vulgar-Freudian and reductive for the density of what has occurred. The child witness is fundamental: as an act of violence it is also an assertion of control, mutilating not the female emblem (or her assumed maleness), but her organ of expression. Touch has been honoured; piano playing has been revealed as a direct notation of self; it is almost an epistemological violence that has been done to the body in the terms the film has so profoundly established.

There is also a further scene of tension between the men. Stewart walks through the night with his musket, and disturbs Baines sleeping. Pointing the barrel of the gun to his cheek, it seems likely he will commit a further atrocity; his driven and homicidal intent seems all too clear. But there is a strange pause, when Stewart considers the face of his rival and says:

> I look at you, your face. I have had that face in my head, hating it. But now I am here seeing it ... It is nothing, you blink, you

have your marks, you look at me through your eyes, you are even afraid of me.

In what might have been a thrill-kill moment in the movie, Campion pulls back. She allows Stewart his broken and deranged humanity and offers the lovers release, not death, from the tyrannical threat of violence. It is a solemn moment, a reminder of what the philosopher Emmanuel Levinas considers the basis of a recuperative ethics, a face-to-face encounter with the despised other that imagines their presence as irreducible and returns to the self a 'gentleness' and a 'responsible freedom'.[63]

8
THE UNCANNY CHILD

One of the visually distinctive forms of repetition in the movie, a shadowing, as it were, an uncanny doubling, is between Flora and Ada. They have pale oval faces, dark hooded bonnets and similar characters. Both make the same *shape*—they *figure* equally and in correspondence. Feisty and assertive, mother and daughter are the primary 'lovers' of the movie. There is a sensuous delight in their identification and it is Flora's petulant and passionate will to be her mother's sole desire, perhaps, which causes her betrayal.

The Piano is a movie that begins by splicing recognition of the founding sensibility of the child with an adult plot—becoming-a-wife. A sexual plot predominates, but there is also, just as fundamentally, a mother-daughter plot and a strong sense in the film of the child both as a subject and a witness, a second heroine, if you will. The sexual agent is also a mother; the daughter is conflated with the mother, visually doubling her, becoming sexualised, and ventriloquising her words. This merging contributes to the augmented emotional tenor of the movie, but also to the eroticism and its attempt to honour the inner life, beyond the body. The visual duplication, striking as it is at times, compounds the on-screen power of both female actors. Rarely has a movie been strung so

AUSTRALIAN SCREEN CLASSICS

Mother and daughter: uncanny doubling.

THE PIANO

elastically between its two remarkable female leads, neither preemptively glamorous or bearing the patina of superstardom. Anna Paquin's performance as Flora deserves its own space in this essay; her role in the narrative, too, is frequently overlooked as critics zoom in with deft prurience to the adulterous triangle.

Flora's role in voicing and translating her mother's signs has made her riskily precocious. The transferential relationship between them, marked in part by (un-Victorian and amorous) physical demonstrativeness, is also implicated in the romanticism of the movie, and in the sublimated search for an acceptable father. It is Flora who asks repeatedly for the story of her father, and she too who supplies a wildly fabulous version to Aunt Morag:

> FLORA: My real father was a famous German composer ...
> One day when my mother and father were singing together in the forest a great storm blew up out of nowhere. But so passionate was their singing that they did not notice, nor did they stop as the rain began to fall; and when their voices rose for the final bars of the duet a great bolt of lightning came out of the sky and struck my father so that he lit up like a torch ... And at the same moment my father was struck dead my mother was struck dumb! She never—spoke—another—word.
>
> AUNT MORAG: Ohhh ... dear. Not another word. From the shock, yes it would be.

This telling—which Flora is shrewd enough to alter as she goes to make it sound believable—is inter-cut after the word 'torch' by a short animated sequence of what looks like a wooden toy soldier raising his arms in alarm and bursting into flames. It's a fascinating cinematographic moment in which an entire *other* visual order of meaning is introduced—one childish, vivid and deeply personal. In Flora's story, *voice* is not just important but am-

The child witness.

plified, enhanced, the sign of her parents' idealised mutuality. And although she is confabulating, she is also convincing Aunt Morag and satisfying herself with a romantic narrative and an explanation of her mother's silence.

Elsewhere in the film, Flora's role is to show what has been repressed, and to enhance the lyrical poetics of the movie, its art-house sequence of redolent motifs. In an early scene, when Flora and her mother return to the beach to visit the piano, she is a dancing and cart-wheeling sprite, expressing for Ada the recovered liberation of play. This scene ends with an overhead shot of a gigantic seahorse created—presumably by Flora—from stones and shells on the beach: it is another brief token of the fabulous (and indeed, fabulous sea-life), another ornamentation of space, a symbol of Flora as a proto-artist, akin in spirit to Ada.

If this might be seem a prettified instance of Victoriana, the development of Flora's character within the movie, her temper

THE PIANO

and her betrayal, disallow any sentimentalising of the figure of the child. She is endowed with a kind of adult fullness and contradictoriness of character. Even when wearing the angel wings, sullied and stained for most of the movie, she exceeds her costume. The scene of swearing, earlier discussed, is disturbing in its rough and ready mixture of meanings. Here a small pretty girl, wearing angel wings, shouts with uncontrollable vehemence that her mother should be buggered. This sexualising is confirmed because Flora is also revealed as a voyeur (watching, as Stewart will, her mother and Baines together) and shown in a scene in which, playing with Maori children, she lasciviously kisses and embraces the trunks of trees. The latter example in fact implies a kind of 'healthy' sexuality, but it is punished by Stewart who insists Flora has 'shamed' the trees and must white-wash the trunks in penance.

Most disturbing is the witness of Ada's mutilation. Flora is spattered with her mother's blood in a moment of drastic and dreadful revelation of Stewart's power, and the cruel act of forcing her to deliver the severed finger—in a grotesquely nightmarish repetition of the earlier errand—results in her hysterical collapse in the arms of Baines. The silence of Ada's response, the gradual sinking, is given alternative expression, performed with jagged misery by the traumatised daughter. This is not to suggest they form a joint character, or substitute each other. It is a more subtle point, that the relationship forms a ramified criss-crossing network of reflection and response. Flora 'tells' her mother by voicing for her, shares a psychical bond wrought by the enwreathing silence, but is also a conspirator in the drama of competing desires. She is a wonderful character, and entirely persuasive.

9

THE THREE ENDINGS

After the sadistic violence done to mother and daughter, and as Stewart, shaken and befuddled, considers the face of his rival, he also voices the peculiar metaphysics of the movie, which swings between propositions of radical embodiment and disembodiment. It is a section of dialogue almost entirely about the status of 'silent' words. Stewart believes he has clairvoyantly 'heard' Ada's voice, directed to him through her accusing stare as she lies feverish, wounded and vulnerable before him.

>STEWART: (softly) Has Ada ever spoken to you?
>BAINES: You mean in signs?
>STEWART: No, in words.
>BAINES: No, not words.
>STEWART: Never thought you hear words?
>>*Baines shakes his head.*
>STEWART: She has spoken to me. I heard her voice. There was no sound, but I heard it here (*he presses his forehead with the palm of his hand*). Her voice was there, in my head. I watched her lips, they did not make words, yet the harder I listened the clearer I heard her, as clear as I hear my own voice.
>BAINES: Spoken words?
>STEWART: No, but the words are in my head. I know you

> think that's a trick, that I'm making it up. No, the words I
> heard were her words.
> BAINES: What are they?
> STEWART: She said, 'I have to go, let me go, let Baines take
> me away. I am frightened of my will, of what it might do, it
> is so strange and strong.'

Stewart recapitulates the mysticism of Ada's silence—her dark talent, her will, her immitigable drive—and in so doing implies he has at last connected with the inner life of his bride, if only in the context of her plea to be released. This may be the rationalising of an act of conscience, or an incorporation of Stewart into the imaginative connection Ada's silence inspires in Baines and Flora. In any case, he is now aware somehow of the link between the tangible and the intangible. He has not grasped Ada's mystery but he has vaguely intuited it. He had seemed uninvolved, detached; now he is addressed, called mysteriously into being to act humanely, to demonstrate compassion and spiritual largesse.[64]

What follows are three tonally and cinematically distinctive episodes which, for the sake of argument, I shall call three endings. *The Piano* does not follow a mono-tracked ride to a romantic resolution; it equivocates, it modifies, it sets in tense juxtaposition contending understandings of what has occurred and what might need to be put at rest.

The first ending is the near-drowning of Ada. After Stewart's encounter with Baines, the next scene is of Baines meeting with Ada to take her away to Nelson. Her expressionless face is ash-white, her hair is loose, she moves like an automaton. There is a bleached, downplayed atmosphere to the reunion; Ada looks lost, reduced, hurt. On the Maori boat (and it is possible, I think, to see the Maori as rescuers once again), the heavy presence of the contaminated piano dominates. It has been roped on board,

AUSTRALIAN SCREEN CLASSICS

The first ending: the near drowning

at Baines's insistence, because he believes he now understands the value of the piano for Ada. But it has become 'spoiled' as Flora translates for Ada, 'a coffin', as the Maori say, and Ada emphatically wants it ejected from her life. Baines is persuaded to ditch the piano in the ocean, and as it slides sideways, with the audible creak and strain of its accumulated history, the camera focuses on Ada's silent response. Here is Campion's view:

> As the piano splashes into the sea, the loose ropes speed their way after it. Ada watches them snake past her feet and then, out of a fatal curiosity, odd and undisciplined, she steps into the loop.[65]

Stepping into the loop drags Ada overboard and plunges her underwater. She descends, a tethered thing, impassive and open-eyed, looking around at the underwater scene. Much like a dream sequence, this descent has a distorted and stylish appeal. The music score is rich, the timing slow-motion, there is a kind of radiance to the other-world becoming gradually apparent. Pearl strings of bubbles rise up in the deep blue water, and Ada's face, in close-up, is surprised and interested. The scene *could* have been an ending—a death by drowning is logically and poetically appropriate, the almost inevitable conclusion to the watery suggestions throughout the movie. But Ada suddenly struggles in the near dark (the timing and depth both seem unfeasibly extended), her boot releases and she rises in her cumbersome garments towards the surface. An underwater shot shows Maori bodies, mostly unclothed, swimming towards her, gathering her in. In a high shot, still in slow motion, still anti-naturalistic, we see Ada break the surface in a bright pattern of lozenge lights and Baines reach over to receive his lover in his arms. The voice-over, in Ada's anomalous little-girl voice, says:

What a death.
What a chance.
What a surprise.
My will has chosen life.
Still it has had me spooked, and many others besides.

It is perhaps troubling that it is an impersonal will, and not a conscious decision, that saves Ada from her own *fatal curiosity*. Supra-personal, mystical, this will of Ada's is again given a motive force, as if it drives through the movie not entirely in her control. *What a death* is also strange, and it is only in retrospect that we realise there has also been a kind of death, that part of Ada remains below the ocean, swaying gently in the currents of a drowning. The death drive, then, is both refused and accommodated. Campion does not execute her heroine in the cause of poetic coherence, but does allow a 'loop' of otherness to exist. The feminist debates around this moment are particularly interesting; as critic Stella Bruzzi puts it:

> Ada decides first to die with her piano and then to live. As the voice-over suggests, this would have been perfect: quintessentially dramatic, feminine and silent; Ada caught in the rope half-exposed, half-engulfed in her clothes, eroticised in death. In wanting to live, however, Ada consigns this image to fantasy, lulling herself to sleep with it, keeping the 'silence' to herself ... [T]o die in the mode of a tragic heroine would have been to succumb to another masculine tradition.[66]

Campion has pulled her soaked, bedraggled heroine from the water, from what is all-too-possible in the Romantic tradition. Ada is offered a future beyond the compelling morbidity of the sea, beyond the familiar scenarios of punishment.

But what are we offered instead? In the second ending, Ada is in Nelson, in a solid-looking house, complete with lace curtains and a white picket fence. It is sunshiny, clean and the frames are brightly lit. In a close-up of Ada's hands playing the piano, we see that an ornate silver prosthesis has replaced her index finger. It produces a disconcerting tap-tap staccato as she plays a conventional, simple tune, not at all the sort of music we have come to associate with her presence. In voice-over we hear Ada say: 'I teach piano now in Nelson. George has fashioned me a metal fingertip. I am quite the town freak, which satisfies.'

There is an ambiguity in the word 'freak', self-ascribed, and in the fact that Ada plays such dreadful music, scarred by her interrupting, inorganic tap. In the next shot Ada, beautifully dressed, her head beneath an opaque black veil, drags her fingertip along an exterior wall, as if she is blind and needing a guiding landmark. The voice-over continues: 'I am learning to speak. My sound is still so bad I feel ashamed. I practice only when I am alone and it is dark'. Thoughout the voice-over we hear Ada practicing her speech: 'Bah ... bah. Deh ... deh'; she is symbolically the child once again, reborn to language.

Cut to a middle shot of Flora, doing cartwheels in the yard, in fresh white ribbons and lacy petticoat; her slow-motion turning implies an idyllic and redemptive scene. The sequence cuts back to Ada, still practicing her phonemes, having created her own dark. Baines then steps into the frame, crosses in front of Ada and flattens himself against the wall. Ada's hand slides over his chest and he catches her as she passes, then he lifts away the black veil and together they kiss. Before the kiss Ada had been practicing the sound 'pah!' She repeats *pah! pah!*, as if, in a none-too-subtle hint, the ideal father has been at last discovered. The tidy reconstruction of what has been lost—finger, voice, piano, lover, father, and the *mise en scène* of domestic bliss, has led many viewers to feel a little disappointed with this section of the movie, seeing in it a loss of the powerful non-conformity by which Ada has been defined.[67] It looks all too unexpectedly pretty, somehow, too contained in another conservative set of conventions: the placated, attractive wife; the uncomplicated, final kiss; the apparent erasure of any remnants of trauma. The black veil, however, is an interesting addition. Although the gesture of lifting the veil and kissing implies a second wedding, here it is an ambivalent unveiling. Ada needs 'the dark' to recover herself; she is 'ashamed' of her voice and without the assertiveness and will that so marked her previous character. Something has been lost.

Yet as Sue Gillett reminds us, 'the seeming closure offered by the domestic ending is only temporary'.[68] The bright Nelson ending cuts to the fantasised image of dead Ada, in penumbral, muffled deep, shining in the dark, still attached to her piano at the bottom of the ocean. It is a memorable image, almost surrealist in import.

Ada's voice once more:
> At night, I think of my piano in its ocean grave.
> And sometimes of myself, floating above it.
> Down there, everything is so still and silent that it lulls me to sleep.
> It is a weird lullaby.
> And so it is—it is mine.

The affirmation of the achievement of a *weird lullaby* at the end of the movie, constitutes an unusual kind of triumph. Ada is not simply living the happy-ever-after dream; she is haunted, and perhaps also reassured, by the persistence of her own clandestine vision. She travels to her vision at night to find a continuity of selves, and the weird sunken sound that is no sound. The concluding lines, still spoken by Ada, are by Thomas Hood:
> There is a silence where hath been no sound,
> There is a silence where no sound may be,
> In the cold grave—under the deep, deep sea.[69]

These lines imply that for Ada there is somewhere, sequestered and private, a state of being that has not been relinquished or forfeited. This is death and not-death, a cinematic moment of meditation, a moment of hallucinatory vivacity and complicated rhetoric, captured in an eerie, and in some ways incomprehensible, image. A sense of calm pervades, a gravity, a sense moreover of the elegiac. There is in this closing a subtle mourning for what can never be represented, a declaration to the audience that all cinema is in the end a phantasm.

NOTES

1. Virginia Wright Wexman, *Jane Campion: Interviews*, Jackson, University of Mississippi, 1999, p. 102
2. Stuart Dryburgh, quoted in Jane Campion, *The Piano: Screenplay*, New York: Miramax Books, 1993 p. 140
3. Jean Epstein, 'The Camera Continues' (1930), in Richard Abel (ed.), *French Film Theory and Criticism: A History/Anthology 1907-1939*, vol. II: 1929-39, Princeton: Princeton University Press, 1988, p. 6
4. If we take the 'wave-motion' of cinema seriously, however, we must concede that the process is radically altered on any second or subsequent viewing of a film. See Noel Carroll, 'Defining the Moving Image' in his *Theorizing the Moving Image*, Cambridge: Cambridge University Press, 1996, p. 65. Hence the instability of interpretations is written into the very ontology and phenomenology of cinema.
5. While a utopia is a fundamentally unreal place, a heterotopia, according to Michel Foucault, is another real space, but strangely other to our own: he cites spaces in cities, like cemeteries, churches, brothels and libraries, and also says that the mirror is a kind of heterotopia. See 'Of Other Spaces', *Diacritics*, Vol. 16, no. 1, Spring 1986, pp. 22-27
6. Richard Allen, 'Female Sexuality, Creativity and Desire in *The Piano*' in Felicity Coombs and Suzanne Gemmell (eds.), *Piano Lessons: Approaches to The Piano*, London: John Libby, 1999, pp. 44-63
7. Wexman, *Interviews*, p. 104
8. Roland Barthes 'Textual Analysis of Poe's *Valdemar*' in Robert Young (ed.), *Untying the Text: A Post-Structuralist Reader*, London: Routledge & Kegan Paul, 1981, p. 153
9. Stanley Kauffmann, *The New Republic*, December 13 1993, in Harriet Margolis (ed.), *Jane Campion's The Piano*, Cambridge: Cambridge University Press, 2000, pp. 189-190
10. Lizzie Franke, Review *Sight and Sound* 3:11 (November 1993), in Margolis (ed.), *Jane Campion's The Piano*, p. 170
11. Stuart Klawans, Review *The Nation* 257.19 (6 December 1993), in Margolis (ed.), *Jane Campion's The Piano*, pp. 188-9. (My emphasis.)
12. The pianos shipped in large numbers to Australia and New Zealand in the nineteenth century were called Broadwoods. In the novel the piano is a Broadwood, in the screenplay

it's a Broadbent and in the movie it appears to be labelled a Woodwood. For an excellent account of the cultural significance of the piano for women in the colonies, see Christine Knight, 'Ada's piano playing in Jane Campion's *The Piano*: Genteel Accomplishment or Romantic Self-Expression?', *Australian Feminist Studies* vol. 21, no. 49, March 2006, pp. 23-34

13. Dana Polan, *Jane Campion*, London: British Film Institute, 2001, p. 37
14. Cyndy Hendershot, '(Re)Visioning the Gothic: Jane Campion's *The Piano*', *Literature/Film Quarterly* 26:2, 1998, pp. 97-108
15. Wexman, *Interviews*, p. 105
16. See Ken Gelder 'Jane Campion and the Limits of Literary Cinema' in Deborah Cartmell, and Imelda Whelehan (eds.), *Adaptations: From Screen to Text*, London: Routledge, 1999 for an interesting study of the text/screenplay differences.
17. Diane L. Hoeveler 'Silence, Sex and Feminism: An Examination of *The Piano*'s Unacknowledged Sources', *Literature/Film Quarterly* vol. 26, no. 2 1998, pp. 109-16. I agree with Ann Hardy ('The Last Patriarch' in Margolis (ed.), *Jane Campion's The Piano*) that Campion cannot be accused of plagiarism.
18. Vivian Sobchack, *Carnal Thoughts: Embodiment and Moving Image Culture*, Berkeley: University of California Press, 2003, p. 65
19. Laura U. Marks, *The Skin of the Film: Intercultural Cinema, Embodiment and the Senses*, Durham: Duke University Press, 2000, pp. xi-xvii. Marks writes: 'Haptic visuality sees the world as though it were touching it: close, unknowable, appearing to exist on the surface of the image.'
20. Sobchack, *Carnal Thoughts*, p. 63
21. Campion, *The Piano: Screenplay*, p. 12
22. This is particularly stressed by Michael King in his *The Penguin History of New Zealand*, Auckland: Penguin, 2003. For other views, see W.H. Oliver and B.R. Williams (eds.), *The Oxford History of New Zealand*, Oxford: Clarendon Press, 1981.
23. Pakeha is a complicated term. Originally 'Pakeha Maori' was assigned to Europeans who formed interracial marriages or adopted Maori custom and had Maori offspring. The term now signifies New Zealanders of European ancestry. It is a term, as Lynda Dyson argues, for a white ethnic identity that makes claims for indigeneity and which avoids the implication of 'white' supremacy. (See Lynda Dyson, 'The Return of the Repressed: Whiteness, Femininity and

Colonialism in *The Piano*', *Screen* 36:3, Autumn, 1995). For a historical account see M.P.K. Sorrenson in Oliver and Williams (eds.), *The Oxford History of New Zealand*, pp. 168-93.

24. King, *The Penguin History of New Zealand*, p. 169
25. Campion, *The Piano: Screenplay*, p. 141
26. Ann Hardy and Jane Roscoe, drawing attention to how centrally the movie relies on black/white opposition for its framing of Maori/White relations, also mount a strong 'whiteness' critique of the movie. See 'Scratching the Surface: *The Piano*'s Post-Colonial Veneer' *Span* 42/43, April and October 1996, pp. 143-57.
27. Autochrome was the colour process invented and patented by the Lumière brothers in 1904. It involved coating the glass plates with a varnish, a thin layer of potato starch, another coating of varnish, and then a gelatine-bromide emulsion, so that the colours were dense, rich and varnished in appearance. For a full definition see Gordon Baldwin, *Looking at Photographs: A Guide to Technical Terms*, Malibu; London: JP Getty Museum in association with the British Museum Press, 1994, p. 10.
28. Campion, *The Piano: Screenplay*, p. 141
29. Leonie Pihama, 'Ebony and Ivory: Constructions of the Maori in *The Piano*' in Margolis (ed.), *Jane Campion's The Piano*, pp. 114-34; p. 128. The phrase 'happy-go-lucky native' is from bell hook's critique of *The Piano* in 'Gangsta Culture—Sexism, Misogyny' in *Outlaw Culture: Resisting Representation*, New York: Routledge, 1994, pp. 115-23.
30. See Ann Parsons on 'The Pursuit of Mana' in Oliver and Williams (eds.), *The Oxford History of New Zealand*, pp. 140-67. She gives an excellent account of how central this notion is to cross-cultural negotiations. A discussion of the role of language is found in Pihama's 'Ebony and Ivory: Constructions of the Maori in *The Piano*' pp. 114-34.
31. Campion, *The Piano: Screenplay*, p. 27
32. Dyson, 'The Return of the Repressed: Whiteness, Femininity and Colonialism in *The Piano*', pp. 267-76
33. This is derived from the screenplay because the full verse is hushed up before the girls can finish their rendition. Campion, *The Piano: Screenplay*, p. 219.
34. Campion, *The Piano: Screenplay*, p. 53
35. Angela Carter, *The Bloody Chamber and Other Stories*, Harmondsworth: Penguin, 1979, p. 39

36. This is the opinion of Stella Bruzzi in 'Tempestuous Petticoats: Costume and Desire in *The Piano*', *Screen* 36:3, Autumn 1995, pp. 257-287; p. 273
37. These are lines adapted from Janet Frame's short story 'Swans'. This beautiful story tells of a childhood memory of a visit to the beach and ends with 'the roar of a secret sea that had crept inside your head forever'. Janet Frame, *The Lagoon and Other Stories*, (1951) London: Bloomsbury Classics, 1991, p. 64
38. Kaja Silverman, 'Disembodying the Female Voice' in Patricia Erens (ed.), *Issues in Feminist Film Criticism*, Bloomington: Indiana University Press, c.1990, p. 313
39. It is interesting to note in this context the echoing role of Nessie in relation to Aunt Morag. This seems to have stunted her individual development.
40. Elizabeth Grosz, *Time Travels: Feminism, Nature, Power*, Sydney: Allen and Unwin, 2005, p. 152
41. Michael Nyman, quoted in Felicity Coombs, 'In the Body of *The Piano*' in Coombs and Gemmell (eds.), *Piano Lessons*, pp. 82-96, p. 92
42. Claudia Gorbman, 'Music in *The Piano*' in Margolis (ed.) *Jane Campion's The Piano*, pp. 42-58; p. 46
43. Sue Gillett, 'Lips and Fingers: Jane Campion's *The Piano*', *Screen* 36:3, Autumn 1995, pp. 277-87; pp. 278-79
44. For a full account of the musical connections see Kristin Thompson, 'The Sickness Unto Death: Dislocated Gothic in a Minor Key' in Coombs and Gemmell (eds.), *Piano Lessons*, pp. 64-80
45. Feona Attwood, 'Weird Lullaby: Jane Campion's *The Piano*', *Feminist Review*, 58 International Voices, Spring 1998, pp. 85-101; p. 91
46. Claire Corbett quoted in Polan, *Jane Campion*, p. 41
47. Carl Plantinga, 'The Scene of Empathy and the Human Face on Film' in Carl Plantinga and Greg M. Smith (eds.), *Passionate Views: Film, Cognition and Emotion*, Baltimore: Johns Hopkins University Press, 1999, pp. 239-255; pp. 249-250
48. 'De-realising ethereality' is Dana Polan's term for describing this implication of blur, weightlessness and female point of view. See his *Jane Campion*, p. 30
49. Campion quoted in Denise Bauer, 'Jane Campion's *The Piano*: A Feminist Tale of Resistance' in Deborah Johnson and Wendy Oliver (eds.), *Women Making Art: Women in the Visual, Literary and Performing Arts Since 1960*, New York: Peter Lang, 2001, pp. 211-26; p. 222

50. Campion, *The Piano: Screenplay*, p. 49
51. See, for example, Cynthia Kaufman, 'Colonialism, Purity and Resistance in *The Piano*', *Socialist Review*, vol. 24, nos. 1-2, 1995, pp. 251-55
52. Polan, *Jane Campion*, p. 33
53. Roland Barthes, *The Pleasure of the Text*, trans. Richard Howard, New York: Hill and Wang, 1975, p. 26
54. See, for example, Lisa Samas 'What Rape is', *Arena Magazine* no. 8, December/January 1983 in response to Kerryn Goldsworthy 'What Music is', *Arena Magazine*, October/ November 1993, pp. 44-46
55. Hendershot, '(Re)Visioning the Gothic: Jane Campion's *The Piano*' pp. 97-108
56. Bauer, 'Jane Campion's *The Piano*: A Feminist Tale of Resistance', p. 220
57. Virginia Woolf, 'The Cinema' in *The Captain's Deathbed and Other Essays*, (1926) London: Hogarth Press, 1950. In the screenplay Ada gives Baines a bloody nose when she slaps him. It would have been a very different kind of kiss with bloody faces.
58. Thanks to Series Editor Jane Mills for the reminder that Lillian Gish's play with bedposts in D.W. Griffith's *Birth of a Nation* (1915) may be a cinematic precedent here.
59. The phrase 'brute matter' is Elizabeth Grosz's. I have in mind here her 'Notes Towards a Corporeal Feminism', *Australian Feminist Review*, 5, Summer, 1987, pp. 1-16
60. In the original screenplay the key is discovered by Baines. It is being worn as an earring by a Maori elder. Baines trades tobacco for the key and takes it to a school house to ask children to read him the message. A chorus of little girls repeatedly read the message to him.
61. Campion, *The Piano: Screenplay*, p. 94.
62. A precise and illuminating account of the soundtrack to this brutal scene is in Claudia Gorbman's article in Margolis (ed.), *Jane Campion's The Piano*, p. 55
63. Emmanuel Levinas, *Totality and Infinity: An Essay on Exteriority*, trans. Alphonso Lingis, Pittsburgh: Dusquesne University Press, 1969, p. 180.
64. In the unmade movie *Ebb*, it is the father figure who is redeemed. 'At the end the father of a family central to the story, the man who was least inclined towards a spiritual adventure, had the most extraordinary experiences. It's for him that the sea returned and his tongue/language began to have a salty taste! He became the sacrificial victim.' See Wexman, *Interviews*, p. 102

65. Campion, *The Piano: Screenplay*, pp. 120-21
66. Bruzzi, 'Tempestuous Petticoats: Costume and Desire in *The Piano*', p. 266
67. Graham Fuller, somewhat tendentiously, has argued that this scene is so unrealistically calm and happy that it must be read as Ada's compensating, pre-death vision. See 'The *Wuthering Heights* of Jane Campion's *The Piano*', *Interview* Nov. 1993, p. 46. Cyndy Hendershot suggests that this is the inauguration of a new form of female subjectivity; a heterosexual relationship without destructiveness is enabled to exist. Hendershot, '(Re)Visioning the Gothic: Jane Campion's *The Piano*', pp. 97-108
68. Gillett, 'Lips and Fingers: Jane Campion's *The Piano*', p. 281
69. The full text is as follows:

There is a silence where hath been no sound,
There is a silence where no sound may be,
In the cold grave—under the deep, deep sea,
Or in wide desert where no life is found,
Which hath been mute, and still must sleep profound;
No voice is hush'd—no life treads silently,
But clouds and cloudy shadows wander free,
That never spoke, over the idle ground:
But in green ruins, in the desolate walls
Of antique palaces, where Man hath been,
Though the dun fox or wild hyaena calls,
And owls, that flit continually between,
Shriek to the echo, and the low winds moan—
There the true Silence is, self-conscious and alone.

BIBLIOGRAPHY

Richard Abel (ed.), *French Film Theory and Criticism: A History/Anthology 1907-1939*, vol. II: 1929-39, Princeton: Princeton University Press, 1988

Richard Allen, 'Female Sexuality, Creativity and Desire in *The Piano*' in Felicity Coombs and Suzanne Gemmell, (eds.), *Piano Lessons: Approaches to The Piano*, London: John Libby, 1999, pp. 44-63

Feona Attwood, 'Weird Lullaby: Jane Campion's *The Piano*', *Feminist Review*, 58 International Voices, Spring 1998, pp. 85-101

Gordon Baldwin, *Looking at Photographs: A Guide to Technical Terms*, Malibu; London: JP Getty Museum in association with the British Museum Press, 1994

Roland Barthes, *The Pleasure of the Text*, trans. Richard Howard, New York: Hill and Wang, 1975

Roland Barthes, 'Textual Analysis of Poe's *Valdemar*' in Robert Young (ed.), *Untying the Text: A Post-Structuralist Reader*, London: Routledge & Kegan Paul, 1981

Denise Bauer, 'Jane Campion's *The Piano*: A Feminist Tale of Resistance' in Deborah Johnson and Wendy Oliver (eds.), *Women Making Art: Women in the Visual, Literary and Performing Arts Since 1960*, New York: Peter Lang, 2001, pp. 211-26

James Belich, *Making Peoples: A History of the New Zealanders: From Polynesian Settlement to the End of the Nineteenth Century*, Auckland: Allen Lane, 1996

Stella Bruzzi, 'Tempestuous Petticoats: Costume and Desire in *The Piano*', *Screen* 36:3, Autumn, 1995, pp. 257-87

Jane Campion, *The Piano: Screenplay*, New York: Miramax Books, 1993

Jane Campion and Kate Pullinger, *The Piano: A Novel*, New York: Miramax Books, 1994

Noel Carroll, 'Defining the Moving Image' in his *Theorizing the Moving Image*, Cambridge: Cambridge University Press, 1996

Angela Carter, *The Bloody Chamber and Other Stories*, Harmondsworth: Penguin, 1979

Peter N. Chumo, 'Keys to the Imagination: Jane Campion's *The Piano*', *Literature Film Quarterly*, vol. 25:3, 1997, pp. 173-76

Felicity Coombs and Suzanne Gemmell, (eds.), *Piano Lessons: Approaches to The Piano*, London: John Libby, 1999

Felicity Coombs, 'In the Body of *The Piano*' in Felicity Coombs and Suzanne Gemmell, (eds.), *Piano Lessons: Approaches to The Piano*, London: John Libby, 1999, pp. 82-96

Lynda Dyson, 'The Return of

the Repressed: Whiteness, Femininity and Colonialism in *The Piano*', *Screen* 36:3, Autumn 1995, pp. 267-76

Jean Epstein, 'The Camera Continues' (1930), in Richard Abel (ed.), *French Film Theory and Criticism: A History/Anthology 1907-1939*, vol. II: 1929-39, Princeton: Princeton University Press, 1988

Patricia Erens (ed.), *Issues in Feminist Film Criticism*, Bloomington: Indiana University Press, c.1990

Janet Frame, *The Lagoon and Other Stories*, (1951) London: Bloomsbury Classics, 1991

Graham Fuller, 'The *Wuthering Heights* of Jane Campion's *The Piano*', *Interview*, November 1993

Sue Gillett, 'Lips and Fingers: Jane Campion's *The Piano*', *Screen*, 36:3. Autumn 1995, pp. 277-87

Sue Gillett, *The Films of Jane Campion*, St Kilda: ATOM, 2004

Kerryn Goldsworthy, 'What Music is', *Arena Magazine*, October/November 1993, pp. 44-6

Pam Goode, 'Foundational Romance, History and the Photograph in *The Piano* and *Far and Away*', *Span* 42/43, April and October 1996, pp. 52-63

Claudia Gorbman, 'Music in *The Piano*' in Harriet Margolis (ed.), *Jane Campion's The Piano*, Cambridge: Cambridge University Press, 2000, pp. 42-58

Suzy Gordon, 'I Clipped Your Wing, That's All: Auto-eroticism and the Female Spectator in *The Piano* Debate', *Screen* 37:2, Summer 1996, pp. 193-205

Harvey Greenberg, Review *Film Quarterly*, 47:3, Spring 1994, in Harriet Margolis (ed.), *Jane Campion's The Piano*, Cambridge: Cambridge University Press, 2000, pp. 184-86

Elizabeth Grosz 'Notes Towards a Corporeal Feminism', *Australian Feminist Review*, 5, Summer 1987, pp. 1-16

Elizabeth Grosz, *Time Travels: Feminism, Nature, Power*, Sydney: Allen and Unwin, 2005

Ann Hardy, 'The Last Patriarch' in Harriet Margolis (ed.), *Jane Campion's The Piano*, Cambridge: Cambridge University Press, 2000, pp. 59-85

Ann Hardy and Jane Roscoe, 'Scratching the Surface: *The Piano's* Post-Colonial Veneer', *Span*, 42/43, April and October, 1996, pp. 143-57

Cyndy Hendershot, '(Re)Visioning the Gothic: Jane Campion's *The Piano*', *Literature/Film Quarterly*, 26:2, 1998, pp. 97-108

Diane Long Hoelver, 'Silence, Sex and Feminism: An Examination of *The Piano's* Unacknowledged Sources', *Literature Film Quarterly*, vol. 26:2, 1998, pp. 109-16

bell hooks, 'Gangsta Culture—Sexism, Misogyny' in *Outlaw Culture: Resisting Representation*,

New York: Routledge, 1994, pp. 115-23

Deborah Johnson and Wendy Oliver (eds.), *Women Making Art: Women in the Visual, Literary and Performing Arts Since 1960*, New York: Peter Lang, 2001

Stanley Kauffmann, *The New Republic*, December 13, 1993, in Harriet Margolis (ed.), *Jane Campion's The Piano*, Cambridge: Cambridge University Press, 2000, pp. 189-90

Cynthia Kaufman, 'Colonialism, Purity and Resistance in *The Piano*', *Socialist Review*, Vol. 24, nos. 1-2, 1995, pp. 251-55

Michael King, *The Penguin History of New Zealand*, Auckland: Penguin 2003

Christine Knight, 'Ada's Piano Playing: Genteel Accomplishment or Romantic Self-expression?', *Australian Feminist Studies*, vol. 21, no. 49, March 2006, pp. 23-34

Emmanuel Levinas, *Totality and Infinity: An Essay on Exteriority*, trans. Alphonso Lingis, Pittsburgh: Dusquesne University Press, 1969

Harriet Margolis (ed.), *Jane Campion's The Piano*, Cambridge: Cambridge University Press, 2000

Laura U. Marks, *The Skin of Film: Intercultural Cinema, Embodiment and the Senses*, Durham: Duke University Press, 1999

Maurice Merleau-Ponty, *The Visible and the Invisible*, ed. Claude Lefort, trans. Alphonso Lingis, Evanston: Northwestern University Press, 1968

Tom O'Regan, *Australian National Cinema*, London: Routledge 1996

W.H. Oliver and B.R. Williams (eds.), *The Oxford History of New Zealand*, Oxford: Clarendon Press, 1981

Ann Parsonson, 'The Pursuit of Mana' in W.H. Oliver and B.R. Williams (eds.), *The Oxford History of New Zealand*, Oxford: Clarendon Press, 1981, pp. 140-67

Leonie Pihama, 'Ebony and Ivory: Constructions of the Maori in *The Piano*' in Harriet Margolis (ed.), *Jane Campion's The Piano*, Cambridge: Cambridge University Press, 2000, pp. 114-134

Carl Plantinga, 'The Scene of Empathy and the Human Face on Film' in Carl Plantinga and Greg M. Smith (eds.), *Passionate Views: Film, Cognition and Emotion*, Baltimore: Johns Hopkins University Press, 1999, pp. 239-255

Dana Polan, *Jane Campion*, London: British Film Institute, 2001

Anne Salmond, *Between Worlds: Early Exchanges Between Maori and Europeans 1773–1815*, Honolulu: University of Hawaii Press, 1997

Lisa Samas, 'What Rape is', *Arena Magazine*, no. 8 December/January, 1983

Kaja Silverman, 'Disembodying the Female Voice' in Patricia

Erens (ed.), *Issues in Feminist Film Criticism*, Bloomington: Indiana University Press, c.1990

Vivian Sobchack, *Carnal Thoughts: Embodiment and Moving Image Culture*, Berkeley: University of California Press, 2003

M.P.K. Sorrenson, 'Maori and Pakeha' in W.H. Oliver and B.R. Williams (eds.), *The Oxford History of New Zealand*, Oxford: Clarendon Press, 1981

Kristin Thompson, 'The Sickness Unto Death: Dislocated Gothic in a Minor Key' in Felicity Coombs and Suzanne Gemmell, (eds.), *Piano Lessons: Approaches to The Piano*, London: John Libby, 1999, pp 64-80

Virginia Wright Wexman, *Jane Campion: Interviews*, Jackson: University Press of Mississippi, 1999

Virginia Woolf, 'The Cinema' (1926), *The Captain's Deathbed and Other Essays*, London: Hogarth Press, 1950

FILMOGRAPHY

An Angel at My Table, Jane Campion, 1990
Holy Smoke, Jane Campion, 1999
In the Cut, Jane Campion, 2003
Passionless Moments, Jane Campion, 1983
The Portrait of a Lady, Jane Campion, 1996
Sweetie, Jane Campion, 1989

L'Arrivée du train en gare de La Ciotat (Arrival of a train at La Ciotat station), Lumière Brothers, 1895
Farewell My Concubine, Chen Kaige, 1993
Rebecca, Alfred Hitchcock, 1941
Suspicion, Alfred Hitchcock, 1941
The Unforgiven, John Huston, 1960
Vertigo, Alfred Hitchcock, 1958
Wise Blood, John Huston, 1979

CREDITS

Release year: 1993

Key Crew
Writer, Director
Jane Campion
Producer
Jan Chapman
Executive Producer
Alain Depardieu
Associate Producer
Mark Turnbull
Director of Photography
Stuart Dryburgh
Production Designer
Andrew McAlpine
Costume Designer
Janet Patterson
Music composed by
Michael Nyman
Editor
Veronika Jenet
Casting Directors
Diane Rowan (NZ);
Susie Figgis (UK);
Victoria Thomas (USA);
Alison Barrett (Aust)
Maori Dialogue and Advisors
Waihoroi Shortland;
Selwyn Muru
Sound Designer
Lee Smith
Production Manager
Chloe Smith
1st Assistant Director
Mark Turnbull

Key Cast
Ada
Holly Hunter
Baines
Harvey Keitel
Stewart
Sam Neill
Flora
Anna Paquin
Aunt Morag
Kerry Walker
Nessie
Genevieve Lemon
Hira
Tungia Baker
Reverend
Ian Mune
Head Seaman
Peter Dennett
Chief Nihe
Te Whatanui Skipwith
Hone
Pete Smith
Blind piano tuner
Bruce Allpress
Mana
Cliff Curtis
Heni (Mission girl)
Carla Rupuha
Mere (Mission girl)
Mahina Tunui
Mutu
Hori Ahipene
Te Kori
Gordon Hatfield
Chief Nihe's daughter
Mere Boynton

Marama
Kirsten Batley
Mahina
Tania Burney
Te Tiwha
Annie Edwards
Roimata
Harina Haare
Parearau
Christina Harimate
Amohia
Steve Kanuta
Taua
P.J. Karauria
Tame
Sonny Kirikiri
Kahutia
Alain Makiha
Tipi
Greg Mayor
Tahu
Neil Mika Gudsell
Kohuru
Guy Moana
Rehia
Joseph Otimi
Mairangi
Glynis Paraha
Rongo
Riki Pickering
Pitama
Eru Potaka-Dewes
Te Ao
Liane Rangi Henry
Te Hikumutu
Huihana Rewa

THE PIANO

Pito
Tamati Rice
Hotu
Paora Sharples
Tuu
George Smallman
Te Kukuni
Kereama Teua

ALSO AVAILABLE

The Mad Max Movies
Adrian Martin

'No other Australian films have influenced world cinema and popular culture as widely and lastingly as George Miller's *Mad Max* trilogy.'

So writes leading film writer Adrian Martin in this sparkling new appreciation of the movies that rudely shook up Australian cinema and made Mel Gibson and George Miller internationally famous.

Martin compares the three movies, sharing his views on which works best and why. In a chapter dedicated to each film, he looks at their critical reception and their themes, examines shooting techniques and provides a shot-by-shot analysis of integral scenes.

Since *Mad Max* roared onto cinema screens in 1979, the films have developed a worldwide cult following and provoked numerous debates as to their meaning: are the films a study of masculinity in crisis, an investigation of good versus evil, a celebration of the Western (with wheels) or a frightening vision of the post apocalypse?

'Max lovers, your definitive fix has arrived.' *Empire*

978 0 86819 670 1

The Barry McKenzie Movies
Tony Moore

When *The Adventures of Barry McKenzie* burst onto the Australian screen in 1972 it created a furore. With 'Bazza' (Barry Crocker), the chundering, Fosters-sucking innocent abroad, Barry Humphries and Bruce Beresford created a foil for the audiences. The movie triggered a riotous sequel, *Barry McKenzie Holds His Own*, and a wave of ocker comedies that celebrate and critique the Australian national character. With irrepressible humour and sharp-witted insight, Tony Moore explores the subversive satire of the films, their influence on his generation, and what they have to say today.

'As Prime Minister I demonstrated my gift for ridicule by granting my only imperial honour to the intrinsically conservative Barry Humprhries. It's time for a book that has fun with the political satire of *Barry McKenzie*.' The Hon. E.G. Whitlam AC, QC

978 0 86819 748 7

Walkabout
Louis Nowra

Nicolas Roeg's *Walkabout* opened worldwide in 1971. Based on the novel of the same name, it tells of two white children lost in the Australian outback who survive because of the help of an Aboriginal boy. The film earned itself a unique place in cinematic history and was re-released in 1998.

In this illuminating reflection, Louis Nowra discusses Australia's iconic sense of the outback and the peculiar resonance the story of the lost child has in the Australian psyche. He identifies the film's distinctive take on a familiar story and its fable-like qualities, while also exploring the film's relationship to Australia and its implication for the English society of its day.

Walkabout, says Nowra, 'destroyed the cliché of the Dead Heart and made us Australians see it from a unique perspective, as something wondrous, mysterious and sensuous. It took a stranger in a strange land to reveal it to us'.

'Louis Nowra's *Walkabout* ... [made me] eager to see the film again ... and my experience of it this second time around was significantly enriched by having read Nowra's book.' *Screening the Past*

978 0 86819 700 5

Puberty Blues
Nell Schofield

'Fish-faced moll', 'rooting machine', 'melting our tits off': with its raw, in-your-face dialogue, Bruce Beresford's film has become a cult classic, just like the novel on which it was based by Gabrielle Carey and Kathy Lette. A coming-of-age film with bite, *Puberty Blues* is set in the 1970s and follows the misadventures of Debbie and Sue, two Cronulla girls angling to break out of 'dickheadland' into the coolest surfie gang. But when they finally muscle their way in, they are disillusioned.

In this lively and honest account, writer and broadcaster Nell Schofield recalls how she won the role of Debbie and what it was like on the set. She looks at the parallels between the film, the book and her own surfside teenage years, and at the extraordinary response the film generated both then and since. It's a story as idiosyncratically Australian as the film that showed everyone who ever had any doubt that chicks can surf.

978 0 86819 749 4

The Devil's Playground
Christos Tsiolkas

Fred Schepisi's film, *The Devil's Playground*, is an intimate portrait of a 13-year-old boy struggling in spirit and body with the constraints of living in a Catholic seminary. It is also the story of how the Brothers cope with the demands of their faith. Made in 1976, this semi-autobiographical film established Schepisi as one of Australia's most talented directors and was one of the first Australian films to be selected for Directors' Fortnight at the Cannes Film Festival.

Christos Tsiolkas invites you to share his twenty-five year journey of viewing, reviewing and re-imagining the film. He remembers his first illicit experience of the film at age thirteen and describes how his views of it changed in later years. As he chronicles the impact of *The Devil's Playground* on the development of his sense of self and of his love of cinema, he also explores the sexuality, politics, history and aesthetics of the film.

It is a passionate tribute to the power and possibilities of cinema.

978 0 86819 671 8